To Malerie,

Because I Tell You the Truth

The truth will set you free!

Suzanne Dorsey

Suzanne Dorsey

ISBN: 1499569491
ISBN 13: 9781499569490
Library of Congress Control Number: 2014909154
CreateSpace Independent Publishing Platform
North Charleston, South Carolina

This book is dedicated to my best friend, the best part of me, the one who opened my eyes, the love of my life, Jason Dorsey.

One of our greatest desires in life is to be understood, yet we hide our true feelings and hope that someone will figure us out.

Because I Tell You the Truth shows how I was able to receive healing in my life. Honesty with myself and with those around me, about what I'm truly feeling, has opened up the door for me to understand who I really am and who others really are also. This has allowed me to see people in a whole new way. Instead of finding a way to make others understand me, it was actually my understanding of others that was most valuable in my life to bring healing.

Honesty was the doorway that brought healing in my life and gave me the vision and strength to forgive others. Holding in my pain only distorted what was really true. I am so excited to share with you my journey, and I pray that at some point, you will be able to see yourself and begin to allow healing in your life.

My intentions for this book are only what God intends. Saying the hard stuff can sometimes be dangerous. People don't always receive what you say in the way you hope they will. I am only obeying God in publishing this book. I never want to say no to God, even when it hurts. I trust that his ways are higher than my ways. I am simply a girl with a story of grace. Don't stop until you reach the end because the score at halftime will never tell you who wins the game. ✱ fantastic

one

Looking in the Mirror

One night, at a weekend camp that our youth group was having, we were playing the story game. You stand in a line, and one person starts telling a story. When it's your turn, you immediately pick up the story where the previous person stopped and make up whatever happens next. If you hesitate at all, you are out. When our youth pastor asked for volunteers, he said, "Ok, I need five people who love to talk." Everyone started saying, "Suzanne! Pick Suzanne! We all know she loves talking!" So I got up there and was excited to be chosen, but the closer my turn came, the drier my mouth became, and I was terrified of speaking. The guy before me finished, and guess what happened next—*nothing*, absolutely nothing! I was blank. Not one thought was in my head except, "Rapture now, please!" At that very moment, I realized even though this was a made-up story, just a game to be played for fun, I felt very, very stupid—stupid like the "dumb blonde" that everyone said I was, stupid like the girl who never stopped talking but had nothing worth saying. This happened eighteen years ago, but I think about it all the time.

As a young girl I was known for speaking my mind openly. At times, it caused problems in school because I didn't always choose the right times to speak. I remember being moved a lot for talking and having to write sentences like, "I will not talk in class." My voice was also used for other things that I am not proud of. I would gripe at my uncles and my cousins for smoking, drinking, or not coming to church. I remember begging them to come to church. I just knew that if they would come, God would change their lives forever. I would cry so hard. I would cry out of fear for their lives with an *honest* broken heart, but I also believed I could make them feel bad enough to do it, if only for me.

After I was able to realize that guilt and manipulation would never change anyone for the better, I was so embarrassed about what I had been doing. I hadn't realized I was doing this before because it was normal in my world. It meant that you cared and that you were doing your part to change people.

In my early teenage years, I tried to be a witness to my friends. I did everything I could to make a difference in their lives. I prayed and cried and begged for them to change. I feared for their lives every day. I cried myself to sleep almost every night, for many reasons but mostly for fear that I would not be able to change any of my friends. I tried to fix them in every way I knew how.

I thought I was doing it right. I was a Christian. I didn't do the sinful things people around me did. I didn't cuss, smoke, or drink. I went to church all the time. I took on a tremendous burden to save the lost. I also did one thing that I didn't realize was working against all of the other things I so proudly did: I criticized everyone who was not like me. Being a good girl means nothing to anyone if you only know how to place guilt on those around you who aren't so good—whether your heart is right or not.

That night at the weekend camp, after my total embarrassment, God began to speak to me in a way I'd never known before. He took that moment to show me that everything I'd heard all my life, everything I was so proud to be, was not his plan for my life—or my mouth. Being so young, I wasn't sure what that meant, but I knew one thing well: I knew the voice of God.

For the next couple of years, I tried my hardest to do what was right and fix all the damage I had inflicted. I tried to show respect for my teachers and leaders. I tried to smile more and complain less, to listen more and speak less. I read my Bible every day. I tried to be more encouraging to my friends every day, telling them that Jesus could take their pain away and they could live in freedom, instead of pointing out everything they were doing wrong. I invited someone to church every single week. I believe, with all my heart, that I did everything I could to reach out to people with a much different attitude—based on what I knew about communication at the time, that is. This is why I had no shame in leaving my senior quote to be read for generations to come. I felt as if I had lost relationships with many friends I had grown up with and most of my cousins, who meant everything to me, either because I wasn't willing to live like they did or because no one wanted an annoying, complaining, manipulating little girl around—family or not. Feeling distant even from teachers whom I had possibly misjudged but honestly not with bad intentions, I quoted these words from Galatians 4:16: "Have I therefore become your enemy because I tell you the truth?"

I was hurt. I loved those people. I loved my cousins, who would later end up in rehab after rehab, go to jail, become fathers but never be allowed to see their babies. I loved my friends, who would later be bound by pain and addictions, living a life they never would have chosen for themselves. I loved my closest friends, whom I said no to every single time they asked me to go to a party and whom I drove for so they could do the things they weren't supposed to be doing. If I could save their lives in any way at all, I was going to do it. I felt like I needed those people so badly, but because I chose Jesus, I couldn't have them. I needed my parents, who did raise me in church and teach me to do the right thing, but I constantly asked myself, "How much can they offer while absolutely hating themselves, each other, and the lives they've been given?" I couldn't say those things out loud, but any other explanation would have been a waste of words.

I found my endurance in thinking they all needed me worse than I needed them. When I was dealing with so much pain of my own, being what they needed was very hard to achieve. I simply decided not to wish for what they could give me and chose to give whatever I could to them. I ran out of strength constantly. I never knew how to keep any for myself.

I had a hard time keeping the pieces of my heart intact, but I loved God! I loved him most because he was the one who was there every single night when my head hit the pillow and I couldn't stop crying. He spoke my language when nobody else did. I had so many chances to run to all the temporary pleasures that filled the world around me, but I couldn't turn my back on the one person who understood me the way God did. I couldn't figure it out: If I was living the right way and not doing what they were doing, then why was I hurting so bad? Why weren't they listening to me? Why was it so hard to go home to my parents and just as hard to leave them every day? Why couldn't I stop fighting with my mom? Where were my friends? How could they deny friendship to someone who loved them so much? What was I doing wrong?

I sang about the joy that was down in my heart, but really all that was in there was pain. Though my life of devotion to God was making a difference in those around me, I couldn't see it because I was only focused on what they were doing wrong. All I felt was fear for myself and for them. Even though God had started dealing with me about my approach to people and their hearts, I was bound by something I could not figure out. I continued living with emotional pain that I was convinced I could never change until everyone around me changed. It was my purpose to change people! Why was I so bad at it?

After I graduated high school, I immediately got engaged to the boy I had claimed since I was five years old. I chased that little blond-haired, blue-eyed boy until he got tired of running and finally surrendered his heart to me! Now that I think about it, that seems pretty strange. He was never the type to be attracted to someone who was desperate for him. Still, after an almost thirteen-year plea from my heart to God, Jason heard God say, "You marry that girl!" Six months later, on December 13, 1997, we were married! We moved to Springfield, Missouri, and started our new life together. My life was everything I had dreamed of, but after a few months of living in a bubble, reality hit. I was eighteen—a grown-up. I was a wife. I was a working-woman. I had to be responsible.

Though these things were exciting to me, and I was living in the center of God's will, I felt trapped by my own secret heart-aches. One night, as my heart was breaking and I couldn't stop crying, I begged God to show me what was wrong. I knew that it wasn't my marriage, my job, or my homesickness. At that point, God started showing me something I had thought wouldn't matter with my new "dream come true" life: he showed me my past. I had grown up with family problems, and I knew that there were some issues I needed to face, but I had no idea it would affect me in this way. I think I had been hoping for "out of sight, out of mind."

two

Admitting What I Saw

At nineteen years old, I was sitting at my desk at the General Council Credit Union in Springfield, Missouri. My desk was surrounded by five offices, where loan officers worked to provide loans for missionaries and ministers all over the world. There was never a moment of silence. The phone was always ringing. If it wasn't ringing, someone was calling me into their office. "Can you bring me that file? Are you done with that file? Have you called them back yet? I need that proof of income! What did they decide? Can you get that phone? We need these filed before you leave. How much is this car worth? Suzanne, I need that copy! What do you mean my loan won't go through? I am a pastor of a church, a credentialed minister, and you can't give me a loan? I can get approved to be a missionary to a foreign country, but you can't loan me two thousand dollars?" I'd have to say, "I am very sorry, sir. Just giving you the message." I was honored to be there but felt overwhelmed most days because I was taking care of the paperwork for five people, pretending my way through most of it just to prove to myself that I could do it.

I rose to the challenge. My biggest trial was the fact that we had to wear panty hose and skirts every day. It was very uncomfortable, but I felt so professional. My co-workers treated me like I was their long-lost daughter who had been raised on a farm and had the cutest little Southern accent because I said "I" like you're supposed to, with *one* syllable instead of five! Every time I was nauseous, tired, or hungry, they had me thinking that I was pregnant. They bought me multiple pregnancy tests and convinced me that even the negative pregnancy tests were sometimes wrong and I could still be pregnant. They made me fat! I gained twenty pounds while I was there. They celebrated every day for any and all reasons. I would have done anything for them, even the mean ole guy from "Wiscaaaanson" who gave me the hardest time of all (he was actually my buddy and someone I really trusted). I did my very best because I knew that God had given me supernatural strength and wisdom to be able to handle the chaos of it all. Most of the time, my determination was enough, but some days it was more than I could bear. Not only was I very young, very broke, and very tired, I was also very bound by things I didn't even know existed in me.

One particular day, I was writing some information down on a file, and my hand started shaking. I then felt a presence that I couldn't explain to you if I tried. Everywhere I looked was a blur, and the only thing I could see was the paper in front of me. Right there in the middle of my little, noisy, chaotic circle, for what seemed like a few minutes, I heard nothing, and the silence around me was the most supernatural kind of stillness I've ever experienced (even to this day). My hand began to write on the bottom of a statement that I had printed out. I couldn't control it—none of the words written were my own. Previously, when it came to supernatural things, all I had known was confusion and fear. This is why I believe the Holy Spirit chose to speak to me through words on paper that I could see with my very own eyes and used ME to write them. When a miracle happens inside of *you*, there's no way to deny it or be afraid of it. I had always prayed not to see any angels, demons, or visions, but God completely shut down the world around me and spoke to my heart without causing fear of any kind.

My heart and my mind had been crippled by a previous experience. I still don't know if it was a dream or if I actually saw an angel in my bedroom, sitting on my dresser. Satan had used that experience my entire life to torment me. I couldn't be alone. He would tell me constantly, "As soon as you walk out of the room, she'll be there. When you look in the mirror, you'll see her. When the lights go out, she'll be there. When you lie down at night, she'll appear. When you answer the phone, you'll hear her voice. You'll never get away from this. You'll always be afraid. If you're afraid of someone who you know loves you, then how could you not be afraid of me? Wait until you see me. I'll be there too! You'll see me in your room when it's dark, and you'll be terrified. Your God might be able to save your soul and protect your heart from me, but you'll always be afraid...*always!*" I couldn't even go to the bathroom without running there and running back to where people were. I always thought the "angel" was following me. Maybe she was, and if so, I am more than grateful now, but for at least 12 years I was tormented with this particular fear.

For years, I never told anyone because the angel I saw was my grandma, who had died when I was one. I couldn't figure out if it was Satan's way of getting in my head or God's way of protecting me all of those years. I do know that in the Bible, 2 Timothy 1:7 (NKJV) says, "For God has not given us a spirit of fear, but of power and of love and of a sound mind." This confused me so much. Why was I so afraid? Sometimes I thought I was crazy, and I sure didn't want other people to think I was dumb *and* crazy, so I just held it in and prayed every day that I wouldn't be scared anymore.

I had not yet dealt with this fear, but God knew how to speak to me, that day at my desk, in a way that I could accept. What a compassionate, creative God! I didn't even know what I was writing until all at once my hand stopped. The silence was gone and my vision came back to normal. I then read what was on the bottom of that statement, and here's what I remember of what it said:

You don't know what this is but you know me. What's inside of you is about to come out, and I am going to use you to bring stillness to a lost and fearful generation. If you will write what your heart tells you, your words will be my words, and there will be freedom in the honest places of your heart.

I began to cry because I knew from that moment on, my insecurities were no longer going to be an excuse to hold inside of me what I didn't know how to let out. I knew that if the Holy Spirit was willing to take my hand and guide it to write exactly what he wanted me to know, the box I had placed God into for so many years had just been broken down for the last time. No matter how smart I was or how dumb, no matter how scared I was or how brave, I was no longer in charge of my purpose. I had always claimed to be "nothing without Jesus." You know why? It wasn't because I believed that with Jesus I could be anything. It was because I believed I was *nothing*. The only way I felt like I was worth anything was because I could hide behind Jesus. There, I didn't have to be strong, smart, or courageous. I began to realize that even my confident claims of Christianity were made out of fear. Fear is what caused me to pray that I would have that "out of sight, out of mind" victory when I first got married and moved away. It wasn't that I wanted to forget my past. It's that I was too scared to remember.

three

Doing Something about It

This was when I started writing. God allowed me to speak my heart through writing letters with a pencil and paper. E-mail, texting, and even cell phones weren't that common yet.

As I wrote what I was feeling, before I was done, God would make sense of it all in ways that I had never even thought of. I used a pencil because when I began to ramble and start drowning in my own misery, God would take me back to the place where I'd left him and taken off on my own. He would then have me erase everything after that point. He started showing me how that whole "Then you will know the truth, and the truth will set you free" (John 8:32 NIV) thing really works.

He also showed me that believing whatever is not true would destroy me, and had been destroying me all along. This included my hidden feelings about pretty much everything I'd ever been through. Not admitting how I really felt inside, good or bad, was a lock on every door that would lead to a clear perspective on life for me. Although I couldn't explain how I felt, I had to try. God used my husband to teach me that. Jason would sit with me for hours and not let me fall asleep without unloading everything inside of me. Even when I couldn't seem to make sense, he would listen and then make sense for me. If I'd married a man who didn't know how to do that for me or wasn't willing to, I honestly think

I might have ended up in a mental hospital—with no family of my own and no future.

Jason forced me to be open and honest with myself. Then God miraculously took me, that girl who couldn't speak a clear thought if her life depended on it, on a journey of writing to show me the way to freedom. Each time that I became overwhelmed with sadness or hurt, I would write. I wrote the hardest things that no one needed to hear but me and God. I wrote those things that only my white teddy bear, covered in mascara stains, and Jesus had heard. By the end of each letter, I would feel like my burden had been lifted. It was always as though I simply needed to admit how I really felt toward that person, and if I could do that, then God would take my hurt and return to me joy. Every time, with every letter, I would sweat and break out in red spots just writing what I felt, even before anyone read it. I felt guilty. I felt disrespectful and like I was going to cause pain. I had been taught that speaking your *mind* makes you tough (which really meant intimidating) and powerful (which really meant prideful) but speaking your *heart* makes you wrong (which really meant someone else may get proved wrong) and disrespectful (which really meant the person would be embarrassed). Is that as confusing for you as it was for me?

I spent my life trying to fix people that I never had the ability to fix, starting with my parents, then the rest of my family, and then my friends. I never knew there was only one person I had the ability change and that it was me. I was the only person I wasn't trying to change. But I didn't know how until I knew it was OK to be honest—not just with myself but with everyone around me. I had overwhelming fear of how people would respond to my letters or poems, but I knew that if God could give me the strength to say it, he would give them the strength to hear it.

Eventually, I began to write when I was overwhelmed with happiness, and I would read what I wrote over and over again because I loved feeling happy. I'd never felt happy without guilt that someone else wasn't as happy as me. It felt so good to read what my own heart was saying and see joy. Just that—*joy*, and nothing else.

Writing became a ministry for me! It was healing for my pain, it was celebration for my joy, it was honesty for my heart, and in all my years of being a "big mouth," it was me actually saying something!

One of the hardest things to do is say how you feel knowing the other person's response will not be what you are hoping for. Even when you've written a letter instead of speaking face-to-face, when you give it to the person who will finally know how you feel, you probably say, "Oh you don't have to read that right now!" You know it will touch the person's heart in some way. Tears may even come. You fear the moment the person looks up. What will the person say? How will the person feel? What if the person thinks I'm stupid? What if the person takes it the wrong way? What if this changes or ruins the relationship that we are pretending to have? Why are we so scared of rejection? But think about it: has being honest with someone ever made you feel worse in the long run? Even if it's the hardest thing you've ever said to another person with a beating heart, do you not feel a hundred pounds lighter once you've gotten it out?

I hope that as I share my most intimate feelings with you, you will see yourself at some point and finally be able to express your-self no matter what you have bottled up inside. If you are an adult, you don't need permission to be honest. If you are a child who has been silenced by fear, by people, or by circumstances, you can write what you aren't allowed to say. Keep your letters in a safe place and pray for the right time to begin giving them out. Trust that God sees your pain and that letting it out, even if only on paper, is making room for God to fill your heart with healing. You also don't have to know how to say it. Just say it. Your peace of mind doesn't have to depend on your circumstances or the people around you ever again.

I would like to suggest a book to help you better understand what true freedom can look like. *Out of the Snare*, by Glenn Dorsey, can change your life. The author, also my father-in-law, has been given a ministry for those who need emotional healing. There are many ministers with hidden secrets, formerly abused (in ways you can't imagine) men and women of all adult ages, younger adults starting out who can't pinpoint the root of their depression and are terrified of raising kids for fear of messing them up, middle-aged businesspeople who have never known a life of courage but are stuck inside of a world where they must be strong, mommies who live with nothing but guilt, dads who hate their dads—you name it, he has seen it.

In a world where antidepressants have become the method of survival for so many people, this ministry is vital! If you think you don't need healing, yet you spend a good portion of your life *trying* to be happy, I suggest this book and possibly even the emotional healing process for you. This process is strictly truth from the Bible and certainly not a man-made concept. It is, however, healing explained in a way that many hurting people would never have been able to see on their own.

four

Finding Identity

My very first healing moment happened with my dad. Looking back now, it makes so much sense why God would start here. Our identity comes from our fathers. For my heart to be honest with anyone, it had to be honest here first.

My dad is a man who grew up in what I would call a very complicated situation. I will not go into details, but let's just say that healthy communication, though the biggest problem, was not the only problem. Just like with all of our families, history gets passed down. Whether or not we choose to change what we believe about what we have been taught is up to us. Some people change their beliefs but not their actions, and that happens when their doubts and fears are stronger than their belief in the truth.

My dad's parents are family people. They value family above all other aspects of life. Going by my experiences with them, they both seem to have come from families who must have struggled with affection and affirmation, but who obviously didn't believe in giving up on each other. So in the middle of raising four kids, in some very hard times, they did what they knew how to do. I feel like there is probably a lot of emotional pain that comes into play from each side, that no one is willing to talk about, making it clear that communication was not the thing that made this family survive. Love? Yes! Devotion? Yes! Open honest communication? Probably about the same as 95 percent of the world...not great.

My dad, both of his parents, and all of his siblings (two brothers and one sister) live within a quarter-mile radius. My dad has always chosen to be responsible for his family. If his family needs him, he is there. He could rightfully have had many reasons for not being there, but it seems as though none of them were ever strong enough to change his devotion. I believe that a part of him lives with the fear that changing his communication patterns, and the way he views life and success, could lead to separation between him and his family. Because of his deep love for each one of them, this is not something he is willing to risk. I admire these things about my dad, but for me, being an only child not having all of those people in my life to consider, this concept is hard to understand. So my dad has spent many years surrendering to the fact that "this is how we do things." We work, we commit, we go to church, and we lie in bed at night with tears in our eyes because we can't quite say what it is we want to say, but man—do we love our family! We just hope and pray that all of the things we've believed for so long will pay off one day so that these trials will have been worth it.

Trials for my dad are many, and I'm not talking about a loss of job, or a sickness that won't go away. I'm talking about deep emotional scars, the kind you use this on: "I forgive you but I sure wish I'd never known you." Being a husband, a parent, a provider without a high school diploma and eighteen years old, feeling like the world is against you, is enough to cause anyone else to give up, but he didn't. I don't remember not seeing my dad in church. I don't remember my dad not being at home at night (except when he worked the night shift). I don't remember my dad missing any plays or holidays or requests for a new puppy. What I do remember, what fogs the best of my childhood memories, is anger. My dad was angry and frustrated a lot. He was tired and depressed and never liked his job or the people he worked with.

He was handsome, smart, talented, funny, and fun! But what I believed about him, he never believed about himself, and that made me sad. I started feeling disconnected, maybe even choosing to a little, but never wanting to. I didn't know how to fix him. I felt helpless. I didn't feel silenced at that time, or like I wasn't allowed to talk about it. I just didn't know that healthy communication even existed. I don't think my dad knew about healthy communication then either.

This is all it seems like we knew about communication: You're mad and you're going to say it. Now I'm going to say what makes me look right and you look wrong, even if I think you're right. Now we are both going to say what we hate about each other, and then one of us is going to leave for a few hours until we cool off. When we come back, we may act like nothing happened, but that depends on if the bills are paid or if the house is clean or if there's any food to eat. If not, then it's going to keep going until finally, one of us is too exhausted to fight anymore. There will not be resolution or forgiveness, only enduring because we *choose* to endure together.

This is not what I knew about communication just between my parents—that's what I knew about it in general. This was normal almost every place I went, on both sides of my family.

But I was the prize! I was the peace. I was the joy. I was the reason people smiled and laughed and made it through the day. So when I couldn't deliver my contribution of happiness, it was a bad day. My dad was there through it all. But as I got older, and I guess emptier, I didn't know how to keep acting happy enough to cover up the pain that was in both of us. Satan used that to put a wedge between my dad and me.

Everyone has issues. Holding them all inside will eat away the truth, leaving nothing but lies. This happened to my dad's dad, and my dad, and then me. The first thing I wrote that I actually gave to the person I was writing about was in June 2001. I wrote about a dream I had and what God showed me about the dream. Then I decided to share it with my dad for Father's Day. I am sharing a copy of the letter with you, but I've added, in parentheses, some thoughts that were not in the original letter.

~

June 2001

The Father He's Always Been

At this moment, I am all wrapped up in a blanket, sitting on my big comfy couch. I just woke up from a dream that I believe has changed my life.

The dream: My husband, Jason, and I were at an annual family reunion. We arrived a little late, as usual, because of a prior engagement. As we walked through the doors—and don't ask me what doors because I'd never seen this place before—we filled our plates and started to search for a seat. Do we sit with the people we don't see often, because isn't that the whole point of a family reunion? Do we sit with the ones we have the least in common with, in hopes of finding something that makes us feel like family? Do we sit with the people who may smell kind of bad because we are afraid no one else will? The list goes on and on, but where do we end up sitting? The same place we sit every year, with our closest family, whom we know everything about.

Well, we were about to sit down, but even in our closest family we still have thirty people. I don't know what this part of the dream has to do with anything, but maybe it will reveal itself later. The entire place was filled with my mom's side of the family, but for some reason my dad's immediate family was there too. Since they were the minority, they all wanted to sit at the same table, but it wasn't possible. I'm sure you can already see it coming. Do we sit all the kids together so that the adults can sit together, or should there be an adult with the kids so they won't kill each other? Well, they all finally found a place to sit, and we were left standing. We aren't kids, but we have no kids, so where were we to sit? For some reason, I was watching my dad the whole time. Whatever table he sat at was where I was going!

We ate our meal, and by the time we all had made four or five trips through the food line, it was time to go home. We talked to a few people, laughed at a few jokes that weren't funny but we knew they had been waiting all year to tell us, said "Good-bye!" and "I love you!" to what seemed like a hundred people, and walked out the doors. Now, everybody knows good-byes are not good enough when said inside the door but instead must be said until you are pulling out of the driveway, and even then you must wave. This is what everyone else was doing, but for some reason, I was just standing there, right outside the doors. My mom and dad were also standing still beside me. Who knows where Jason was?

At that time, out of nowhere, this bed appeared right in front of the doors, and we thought, "Hey, let's sit down!" Never mind the fact that this bed just appeared out of nowhere. You know how dreams are. So my dad and I sat down. My mom chose to stand. She must have caught on that something was kind of weird about the whole thing. Well, anyway, we were all just talking when I decided to grab my dad's head and throw him back. I started laughing, and he said, "Oh, you think that's funny, do ya?" Then he body-slammed me and I tried to knock him down. I was standing on the bed, jumping around and fighting with him like I was five years old. I was laughing so hard and had him pinned down great when the back of a couch appeared in my face. It took me a second to realize I had just woken up.

This dream would not sound very deep and meaningful to most, but for some reason it meant the world to me. I was lying there on the couch asking God to help me define this dream.

This is what he showed me. Even though most people saw my family as a great family who went to church together every Sunday, always looking our best and always adding brightness to the room, that was really the only time we were together.

My mom and dad didn't have much in common or much they agreed on, so they typically went about their own business separately. I would always go with my mom. Being a young girl, this seemed normal to me. As I started getting older, those circumstances didn't seem so normal anymore. I didn't really understand the things that were happening in my life. Satan started putting lies in my head, and I didn't know how to get them out, so I started believing them.

(There was a huge part of me that felt separated from my dad. I'd always wondered why. I didn't realize how this was affecting me until my joy was continually being taken away even though my current situation was so great—being married and away from the daily struggles I'd always had at home. What I believed about my dad was not that he was a bad person or was in any way neglectful, but that he was choosing not to make it work with me or anyone else. I thought, because of all I'd seen, that he was just too stubborn to change. I would later find out many reasons why he couldn't bring himself to change, and with the way his world had been designed around him, he never believed it was even possible.

People invested in him, prayed for him, gave him revelation and hope. They gave him, what seemed like, obvious answers and opportunities to experience the freedom they felt, but they had no idea what was eating him up inside—what none of those answers would change. Their efforts to help only made him irritated and embarrassed. Satan had filled his head with so many lies about himself that even help looked like pain.

The saddest thing about a lack of communication is that we are clueless about what the people around us are really feeling, and because of that, we are clueless about the fact that we don't have to keep feeling the same way toward them. I honestly believe my dad could have felt that freedom if he had been willing to be honest with his heart. Not one time did I ever think to hold this against him. I just never understood how to look past it. Because my heavenly father loves me even more than my earthly father does, I believe that, again, God knew what truths I needed to hear about my dad, and only he could tell me in a way that I would accept.)

Today, God told me that my dad has always worked hard. He has never depended on someone else for what he is responsible for. Because of the man he was when I wasn't even looking, I am so many things that I am today. Even though the hours spent together were not nearly enough, that did not change his love for me. Though he may have been many of the things I had been told he was, that *doesn't* mean it was who he wanted to be.

(Do you have any idea what kind of release from pain this gave my heart? I knew my dad was a great man, but I could never accept the fact that I couldn't change him or that I didn't have to change him to feel his love. When God showed me my dad's heart, I was able to put that in front of his actions. I never saw him the same way again.)

My dad is different from anyone I know. He can make a joke out of anything and have you laughing until your stomach hurts. He can also look at you with eyes that cut deep into your heart, and you know exactly what he's thinking without him saying a word. Maybe that's just with me, but it seems so obvious.

(You know how deaf people naturally use their other senses in a much more powerful way than those who can hear? I believe that children who don't hear many words from the people they need most, naturally learn to understand those people without words. They listen to what they feel, not what they hear.)

My dad can play almost any instrument, when he takes the time to teach himself. Every time I saw him play sports, he was always the best player on the team. He can, somehow, save a few dollars a week and build a new house, debt free! He has always fixed his own cars, motorcycles, and four-wheelers. He built tree houses. Never the plain kind—he built the kind you would see on TV! Every kid he encounters thinks he is the one to cling to. For someone who is so against himself, he sure has accomplished a lot. I've never seen him try something and not be able to do it!

He is not only all of those things; he is also one of the greatest Christians I know and has held on to God through every trial in his life! Sometimes he only did that out of fear. Sometimes he only did that out of respect, but he did it! When he didn't feel it, want it, or even believe it, his heart was strong enough to tell his brain to take a backseat. On both sides of my family, I have seen people run to their outlets (which included drugs, alcohol, cigarettes, divorce, antidepressants, clubs, and totally selfish ambitions) but I've never seen my dad, or my mom, do any of those things. With the lies in his head and all the doubt in his mind, how did he stay so strong? He's really just amazing! I'm starting to realize the reason he was never really outgoing is because he would've made everyone jealous of how awesome he is!

I'm sure there are people who have looked at my relationship with my dad and felt sorry for me. At times, I have definitely felt sorry for myself. But through this dream, God showed me the fun times we had that Satan tried to cover up, and that my crippled heart chose to forget. The part of my dream where I was wrestling with my dad made me start thinking of all the times that my dad would wrestle with me at Granny's while watching Rowdy Rowdy Piper and Jake the Snake. He would take me to the car races and listen to me gripe and complain about how it was too loud and too cold, but he would keep on taking me over and over again. I remembered all those times he would say, "No more dogs!"...then bring me one home the next week. God showed me the times my dad *had* spent with me where he *was* the man he wanted to be!

(You know, God didn't have to do that. Many people grow up without a father these days, and God is enough for them. Many people rest in the fact that they do have a father in God. If God was selfish, he could've just fulfilled my heart's desire, but he loves me and he loves my dad. He created us for each other. He created fathers so that we can understand his love. When Satan tried to tell me that my dad was not enough, God said, "Silence, Satan. That's not the plan!")

Then God showed me the reason I didn't care about sitting with anyone but my dad at the reunion. Of all the family I had, on both sides, even though my life was spent more with those people than with my own dad, compared to my dad, they meant nothing to me.

No one could ever take the place of my dad in my life. I respect him as much as a person can respect someone. I love him because he knows how to say, "I love you," with more than just his words. He is consistent, stable, and honorable. I know he loves me with the most intense kind of love there is. He hardly even sleeps at night because he thinks about me so much and prays constantly for the very best for my life. All of my life, he has worked in pain (physically and emotionally) to be the best person he knows how to be. I can honestly say that the father he's always been is the father I hope he'll always be!

Happy Father's Day, Dad! I love you with all my heart!

Love,
Suzanne

~

My honest heart, the one that shows up when my subconscious takes over and I can dream without restrictions, wanted my dad more than anyone! Even if he couldn't always give me what a confident man of God who fully understood communication could have given me, he gave me all that he could. *How many dads actually do that*? Looking back, I would have chosen communication over anything material every time. But because that wasn't something he knew how to give, the fact that he gave his best to me, in every way he *did* know, showed me his true heart. God was able to use that to refill the gaps in me that Satan had filled with lies. *Only God* could have shown me those truths. By choosing to believe them, *only I* could have changed the way I felt about my dad.

Circumstances blur our perspective, sometimes for years. Only if we refuse to see people through God's eyes, will misery continue to be the story of our lives.

Many people have not found identity in an earthly father, even through the eyes of God. If this is true for you, then say how you really feel about God himself. Tell him that you don't understand him. Tell him that you're hurting. Tell him that you're mad. Tell him you need a Father! Tell him that you hate your life and that you wish things were different. He will understand. He will not be mad. Let him in, he will creatively, compassionately, and completely heal even you!

five

Finding Purpose

Jason graduated in December 1999, and we moved to Heber Springs, Arkansas. This would begin our first full-time ministry position. We were honored to be the youth pastors at Heber Springs First Assembly of God. There were about ten kids in our group when we started. One little girl in particular grabbed hold of my heart and wouldn't let go. Her name was Jessica. This part of our lives was so special. I was only twenty years old and pretty much clueless about how to be a youth pastor's wife. Having plenty of my own issues to work through, I found every day to be a miracle. My "nothing without Jesus" mentality was in full effect. I basically told God, "I know how to do three things: love you, love Jason, and love people. Beyond that, I'm all yours. Do what you will!" It turns out those three things are actually all it takes, if you can do them for *real*. If you fake it, you fail. If you give them your honest heart, no regrets! So that's what I did.

Beautiful, sweet, very affectionate, but hurting little Jessica stole my heart. We had only been there about nineteen months when God called us back to our hometown, and we still love every one of those kids. I think about them every day. When we announced that we were leaving, Jessica took it the hardest. She had identity issues and wanted badly to fit in. She started dealing with small things around this time—not major issues, but the kind that you know can easily turn into big issues. She trusted me and needed me, so I felt like it was time to be completely open and

24

honest with her. When you can no longer give people your time, you can still give them your heart. This is what I wrote and gave to her before we left.

~

July 2001

Expect, Pray, & Believe!

I have been here for one year and seven months. From the first time we met, I felt that there was going to be something very special between us. I have always tried to show you why being a "sold-out" Christian is so important. I know that I haven't always said what you wanted me to say, but if I had done that, you wouldn't have needed me. My answers and comments were not always exactly what was right, but I tried very hard to filter everything I said and did through God. That way, we both could live life with as few regrets as possible. I know that I could've done better in the short time I was here, but this is actually my first time to be in ministry, and I'm learning everything as I go. I have tried to be honest and fair with everyone. I have tried to love and appreciate something about each of the students in Frontline.

Loving people has not been hard for me to do. It's the leaving that hurts so much. I want you to know that my body is leaving but my heart is not. I don't really know how to answer questions like, "Are you going to love them more than us?" or "What's going to happen to us now?" or "Why did you only stay for a year and a half?" I honestly don't know how I can even love another group of students as much as I love you. I have no idea what God has in store for Frontline. I can't tell you why we only stayed this long. But I do know this: *God is in control!* Life is not for us to figure out—it is for us to lay down. We were created to tell people about Jesus and to praise him. We live so that someone else might live!

When I was in school, I couldn't care less about anything my teachers said. It made me so mad that my teachers were wasting my time showing me how evolution happens, when I was trying so hard to convince people to believe in God. I had a bad attitude about school. I thought it was stupid, and almost everything about it made me mad. Now that I'm older, I realize how stupid I was for having that attitude. I missed out on all that knowledge that I really did need in life. I don't wish I could go back, but I wish, so badly, that I had listened when I had the chance. Although I didn't make straight As, Bs, or even Cs, there is one thing I do not regret about my life. I do not, nor will I ever, regret selling out to Jesus, no matter what the cost! Everything in life, ultimately, is meaningless! Yes, I wish I could name the presidents, or at least the first five, but what good would it be if my soul did not cry out to Jesus every day for the people who are dying and going to hell? I had no desire to go to college or better myself academically, but I did have every desire to see the lost saved. It's wrong to use that to justify my lack of effort in school, but I didn't realize that's what I was doing until now because I see you doing the same thing. I now believe that all children of God should do *everything* to the best of their ability, and that if they don't, it reflects on what we say is true of Jesus.

Jess, I realize that it's hard to be a Christian. I know what people say about you. I have lost the friends, the popularity, and the cool factor. I have cried myself to sleep over boys. I have stood in front of a mirror for three hours trying to achieve that look that it seemed like everyone had but me. I've been there so many times, and it always came down to this one thing. When the makeup comes off, and you're tired of pretending to be someone you're not, ask yourself this: "Who is standing with me now? Who is holding my hand? Who still loves me just the same?" Then you will have your answer as to who you are, whose you are, and what life is really about. Your friends can't take Jesus away from you. Your friends can't take you away from Jesus. It's your choice, and if you choose Jesus, you can't choose the world too.

Your life should not be about choosing to listen to the hottest new song that's out just because you love it and you *can*. Your life should be about choosing a song that doesn't break the heart of God and that can bring you closer to him. Any other choice, though it may seem cool and popular, will only leave you with temporary joy because at the same time you are feeling accepted by the world, you are pushing the truth out the door to make room for lies. We choose to feel depressed when we listen to depressing songs. We choose temptation when we listen to songs that tell us lies about what our body was created for. We choose anger when we listen to songs that tell us we have a "right" to be angry. All of this leaves us empty. When we are empty, Satan runs in with his bucket of lies, and we aren't strong enough to handle it or get rid of it.

It's super cool to have lots of guys standing in line for you. That makes you feel like you have something no one else does. You know what it means? It means you do! They know it and they want it. If you give that to them because of how awesome it feels to be the one they all want, then when God brings the one person who was created to love you forever, you won't have all the pieces of your heart to give him because they will already have been given away.

I don't expect you to do exactly what I did or be exactly what I am because God has his own plan for your life. I only expect you to love Jesus no matter what it costs you! I expect you to listen to God when he tells you something and do it or don't do it. I expect you to tell people no when it's needed, and I expect you to take as many people to heaven with you as you can.

I pray that God will save your family members who aren't saved, not only for their sakes but for yours as well. I pray that God will help you through every trial in your life. If you let him, I know he will. I pray that God will bless your life and give you the man of your dreams and that the man of your dreams will be the man that God wants you to have.

I believe that God can take away all of the hurt in your life. I believe that God created you for a purpose and knows exactly where you are and what you're going through. I believe that you will grow up to be the woman of God that I know you can be. And last but not least, I am here for you, I will always be here for you, and I love you with all of my heart!

Love,
Suzanne
~

Jessica had one of the most beautiful and determined hearts of any fourteen-year-old girl I've ever seen. She was passionate. She was also very sensitive and easily hurt. She wanted desperately to be loved by the right person, and to be loved forever. I asked her recently to tell me what happened after we left that church. I keep up with her as much as I can, and I know the rest of the story, but I loved seeing it on paper. She was happy to let me share her words with you. This is what she wrote:

"Since you've left Heber: Well, after high school I went to Arkansas State for two years. November 2007, I met the man of my dreams on eHarmony. July 4, 2008, Jeff asked me to marry him, and of course I said yes! March 7, 2009, we got married. During the first year of marriage, we had planned on me taking a break from school. We learned a lot that year. He already lived in Missouri, so after our wedding I packed up and moved here with him. The week of our one-year anniversary, we found out I was expecting our first child. October 23, 2010, we welcomed our baby girl, Aubri Lanai, into the world. Since we've been married, our ministry has been working alongside the staff of our church with the youth. Jeff sings on the worship team. Our heart is with the youth...they are the next generation. Our daughter is almost three, and I'm back in college finishing my nursing degree. In May 2014, we will welcome our second child!"

I'm so very proud of her and the way she used every ounce of pain, passion, and dreaming to believe that her someday, in the hands of God, would be better than her current reality!

six

Finding Courage

As you read this next letter, written to my mom, keep in mind that everything written has a time and a season. I love my mom, and besides my husband, she is the best friend I've ever had. She has spent her entire life giving me everything she possibly could. She has been through more in her lifetime than I will ever know and deserves every good thing that this life has to offer her on top of all the rewards of heaven. My mom knows how it feels to be rejected by many people and, in some ways, even her own daughter. You may ask yourself, "How could a person say these things to her own mother?" I want you to realize something: your mother should be the one person you can be totally honest with. Whether or not she was strong enough to create the kind of environment for you where you were able to share your feelings, she is going to love you, no matter how bad it hurts to hear the things you need to tell her. Most of our issues in life stem from the relationship we had with our parents. I had great parents—they loved me most and did everything they could to give me the best life possible—but they hated themselves in ways I could not understand, and that was very hard for me.

In this book, I am not trying to tell you that I have all the answers for everyone in my life and yours. I realize I haven't always said what was best to say. What I do know that is absolutely true is that if I've been hurt and I don't tell the person who hurt me, I will *never* have an honest relationship with that person.

For some people in your life, that's OK. <u>Forgive them and let them go</u>. For people whom you were meant to be with, even when they don't know how to accept an honest relationship, you must *force* honesty and unfortunately go through the fire of that process. I have talked to many people who say that this is a problem for them. They grew up with very stubborn families who—there is no other way to say it—let pride stand between them. They were oblivious to the fact that showing their weaknesses revealed their strengths. They only did this because that's what they learned to do. They may have realized it once they were grown, but they haven't been strong enough to stop the fake relationships and force real ones.

What happens to the children in these families is they grow up not being allowed to share their true feelings because it will, in turn, show other people's flaws. So they stop sharing feelings at all. Positive feelings make them look weak. Negative feelings cause conflict. The weird thing is that the babies in these families are treated with every kind of love imaginable. It's like the bottled-up love that no one will talk about has to come out somewhere, so when the children are between the ages of birth and about four years old, there is no lack of communication with them. Once children become old enough to have a real voice, they are no longer permitted to say how they feel. It's not like people walk around shoving socks in everyone's mouths, but it is like walking on eggshells. It's a guessing game as to what will be offensive. It's "my way or the highway." It's as if no one deserves to feel what they feel unless they feel the same thing as everybody else in the family, when in reality, no one else feels the same way either, but they are too scared to say that. If someone's thought is more than two sentences long, it will not be fully heard. Listening without a plan for diversion could get too deep. It hurts there. Everyone just accepts the fact that there is too much pain to clean out, so it's better to leave it inside. To justify their obviously scarred hearts (which can't be hidden because of their public acts of impatience, anger, and pride), they claim that *their* normal *is* normal.

Then those children become adults. They start to think for themselves. They then realize they had something to say all along. Because they never learned how to communicate without fear of the result, now most of their relationships with their family members are simply based on the fact that they were raised together or that they have the same blood. Their everyday physical lives no longer include those people, and now they are forced to continue those relationships based only on communication—*which they know nothing about.* It's either that or let them die completely. It's hard enough to face that reality when thinking about their relationships with friends, cousins, aunts, uncles, and grandparents, but it's much harder to face when it comes time to think about their parents.

How do you communicate with a person you've never communicated with? How do you live as an adult and make choices when all you've known to do is listen and obey? How do you build relationships with other adults when all the relationships you've ever had were simply the outcome of putting your body in the same room as someone else and finding something to disagree on, just to have something to talk about? How do you get close to people when you aren't allowed to tell them how you really feel and when you don't know how to accept how they really feel? It's complicated. It gets more complicated when you are the child of that kind of child.

I always thought, you know, if I had really sorry parents who didn't care anything about me, it would be so much easier to be straight-up honest with them, but my parents think I hung the moon. They did everything they could to give me a good life. They aren't bad people—they just had no idea how badly I needed to be honest with them and how badly they needed to be honest with me. That wouldn't have proved that we were losers. It would have opened up a door for an honest relationship between us all, allowing us to focus on the good that was hidden down deep and throw the other junk away.

They encouraged my honesty. They loved my seemingly confident personality. But when it came time to be honest with *them*, it was never received. How do I go back now? How do I respect them and, at the same time, tell them how hurt I was all those years that they worked so hard to make me happy, when the only thing I *ever* wanted was for *them* to be happy?

I resented both of them, in some ways, for not fixing what was broken. I didn't want their attention. I didn't want their hard-earned money. I didn't want their advice and ideas until they could somehow find a way to be honest with themselves and stop living such depressing lives. I thought the problem was my mom not being able to hold her tongue and my dad not being able to choose happiness. That's what I saw. If I'd known where all the pain and hurt were coming from when I was younger, if they'd been able to figure out and then say where it was coming from, and if I'd been able to say how their pain was making me feel, I honestly believe we all could have sat in the same room for more than twenty minutes without having knots in our stomachs from fear of what the others were about to say or how they would say it.

My dad was really good at showing my mom's flaws, and my mom was really good at showing my dad's. I was never on anyone's side. I saw everything about my mom that my dad saw, and I saw everything about my dad that my mom saw. Something that neither of them seemed to notice very often was the good stuff. To remain neutral, I told myself the good outweighed the bad on both sides. It made me furious that neither of them could stop fighting and just do that too. They used extreme amounts of effort to look for the best, but I could see the underlying thoughts in both of their minds that never allowed them to see each other clearly.

If you know me at all, this will sound completely unlike me, but when I was younger—much, much younger (probably five to seven)—my grandparents had a cat. One day, I was so mad, and honestly I don't remember why, but all I could think of was to take that cat by the tail and hit his head against a brick wall. So I did. The cat lived and I never did anything like that again. My point is that when a child is full of pain, the pain turns to rage. It doesn't matter how old or how aware you think your children are—their minds cannot protect their hearts. You can hide your arguments all you want to, keep putting on your happy face. If you stop for one second and your children get a glimpse into your eyes, you better have some peace to show them, or they will become just like you. You never have to hide a disagreement from your children as long as, in the middle of it, you teach them how to resolve conflict the right way. Stop blaming it on someone else. As a parent, what *you* do and what *you* say will never be someone else's fault.

I'm about to be totally honest with you—and I never thought I would say this, but I know God wants it to be said for a purpose. When I was younger and feeling like I was about to explode with anger, I used to look in the mirror and whisper all of the things I would have said if anyone had ever asked me what I really thought.

After I began listening to the honesty inside of my heart, it became overwhelming how badly these relationships needed to be fixed. God started showing me that it wasn't that I had a bad life or bad parents, just really bad communication. It wasn't that I needed different parents; I just needed to be honest with the ones I had. If that was the problem, then there was only one way to fix it.

My goal for sharing this very personal letter with you is for you to see that *as hard as it is*, you can be honest. If you continue with a false relationship because you are afraid of what honesty may bring, it will eventually become a relationship you despise and only make both of your lives harder.

If you fast-forward a few years, you will begin to see that my mom and I had started our journey to a good relationship that was based on the love that has always been there without the unspoken truth getting in the way. From the first time I was honest, I could see healing taking place. Yes, we still have disagreements from time to time, but now we respect each other's choices and aren't threatened by the fact that we are different! I'm not promising that your mom will understand the way mine did, and it even took my mom a few days to respond, but she also wrote a letter to me. You may think that's pretty lame for a mother and daughter, but courage is courage in whatever form it comes. I've heard a lot of criticism toward those who text or write what they cannot say. I agree that abusing that alley of communication is cowardly, but never overlook the importance of the honest heart coming through just because the words are not face-to-face. Isn't it true that we all use whatever amount of courage we have just to get us to a place where maybe we'll have more courage? Just because it's not the same for you as it is for someone else doesn't mean that person is less of a man or woman than you. If honesty is only read, and never heard, in your lifetime, it is still healing. Receive it and give it...even if you have to go first!

I didn't always understand what I was feeling, but I knew that when something hurt me, it was real. We can choose to either deal with it and hurt for a moment or live a lie and hurt forever.

~

October 2001

Mom,

I had to write this because I knew it would never come out right if I didn't. Today at the Fall Festival, when I told you to leave that mom alone and you got mad at me, this is what I wish I could have said: Mom, so many people in this world do things that I don't understand. People say things that make me mad and do things that get on my very last nerve. I realize that nobody is perfect and that I'm not even the judge of what perfect is, but I need to tell you some things about me so that you will understand why I feel so unable to be me around you.

There are three people in this world that I feel responsible for: my husband, you, and Dad. I was conceived in sin, but God used what Satan meant for bad to make good. God knew everything that was about to happen in your life and Dad's, and he gave you me. Although I don't always understand my daily purpose, I understand that I am a child of God and he will take me where he wants me to go. Some days I make a difference for the good and sometimes for the bad. Sometimes I help people and sometimes I hurt people. But in the middle of it all, the thoughts that consume me are almost unbearable because I don't know how to focus on my purpose while worrying so much about yours.

Here are my everyday thoughts: I wonder what my mom's doing today. I wonder what she's thinking about. I bet she is happy today because the sun is out and it's pretty good weather, not too hot, not too cold. Oh, and it's October, so she will get to decorate for fall. She loves fall. I bet she'll be happy most days this month. I wonder if she is in a good mood today. I sure wish she knew how to think about her own life instead of always focusing on what everyone else needs to change. I know she could be happy if she would just do that. I wish she knew how to be content. I wish that what she had were enough. I wish she could stay happy. I would give anything to know how to make that happen for her. When she calls me today, I wonder if she will listen to me, or if she will hide all of her pain with constant one-sided conversation so that nothing else gets in. I don't know how to fix her. I wish she were made like me and didn't have to worry about her weight. I wish I could be fat and she could be skinny. I would do that, if it meant her being happy.

These are my thoughts, Mom. This is what I know to think. Everything else seems to matter at the very bottom of the scale of importance to me. I was raised to care. I was taught that if for one second I acted like I didn't care, I would be criticized for not caring. You tell me to stop worrying about you and your happiness, but you are the one person who has always said that you couldn't survive without my concern. Maybe it's not true now, but it always was in the past, and until I see a difference in the way you communicate with me, I will have to believe that it's still true. And the fact that I can't say any of these things to you without an argument or feeling like I'm going to puke makes my life so hard. I am happy. I have what I prayed for and what I believe God has for me, but I can't figure out how to get through to the one person who lives every moment of her life for me. How can you love me so much and hate everything I have to say?

For eighteen years I lived with you and Dad. I learned to go to church, pray before I eat, pray before I sleep, brush my teeth three times a day. I learned my hair must look good, my clothes need to match, I need to stand up straight and arch my back, I need to speak my mind and not let anyone control me, but when I come home, I need to hold everything in, unless I'm willing to fight it out, and I need to understand that some things you just don't talk about. I will be loved and taken care of, and someone will always have my back. Life is mostly chaos but church is our refuge, and someday Jesus will take us to heaven, where our trials will be no more. We just have to stay faithful!

I realize that everything you taught me was out of love and out of determination to have me be the best I could be. I understand that you did what you were taught to do and I have become mostly what you wanted me to be. And even though it's embarrassing to me, you don't know how to not talk about me to every person you see. You love me...no doubt! But things still aren't quite right between us.

Although I am mostly what you have created, our personalities cause conflict, and this is why. When you tell people how you think they should take care of their kids, it embarrasses me. People who aren't asking for advice only receive corrective advice one way—negatively. You may be right that they shouldn't have their kids outside in such cold weather, but it's not up to you, and telling them what you think about it just causes awkward moments for us all. Many kids have endured many cold days and made it. Please stop telling people what they should do. When you finish my sentences or interrupt me, it makes me feel like what I'm saying is not important. You want me to have my own mind and be a strong woman who knows how to speak clearly, but you won't let me think without feeling the need to finish my thought. I know you, as a mother, are just trying to help, but it doesn't help me. It makes me feel inadequate. You get mad at me for not answering or responding immediately, and that makes me not want to respond at all. I have to think about my answer before I say it. I need a second to do that. I'm not trying to ignore you. I hate meaningless conversation for the sake of talking. It's abnormal, I realize, but it's who I am. I like to talk about feelings and answers to life and how to get from one place in your life to the next. I'm not a small-talker. I'm a thinker. And though my biggest fear in life is that you don't have someone who understands you and is there for you like a great friend should be, the fact that you are very defensive about people showing you things you may need to change a little makes me worry that maybe you couldn't handle close friends, because that's what they tell each other.

Mom, I know you wish things would just feel like they used to between us, but that can't happen because neither of us is who we used to be, and I am so thankful for that. We are realizing that life is not all about you for me and me for you. I know I will never be all that I want to be, but my entire life is about change, and my life keeps getting better and better. That is what I want for you. The hardest thing for me to do is talk to you about what I really want to say because I know it will either make you mad or hurt your feelings, and you won't understand. I know that it's hard to feel like you should change your reactions just to have a better relationship with someone, because you weren't trained to believe that. In our family, there is a mentality that if God wanted us to be different, he would have made us that way. But what we *all* fail to realize is that is only a way to justify our actions and reactions without admitting we should change them.

I really want the rest of our lives to be better than the last twenty-two years, and I know they can. I'm sick of getting mad at you and I'm sick of you thinking I'm a hateful person who never responds the way you want me to. I want you to know that I love you and our relationship does not have to be like this. I can't let you live the rest of your life and never say what I feel, because I know it would help if you could hear my heart. You may be asking yourself, "Why is my daughter the only person telling me these things if I really need to hear them?"

Well, maybe it's because I love you *that* much and want to see you happy with your life more than anyone else who's ever known you! Maybe it's because I'm the one who sees all sides to you. I'm the one who watches you smile and laugh and then go home and cry. I'm the one who listens to you say the things you don't mean, even to me, and who knows how to translate it all to fit inside of my heart the right way—*me*, your daughter, the one who was made inside of you, who will never give up until I see a real smile that doesn't turn into a frown every time it rains. *I am the one who wants happiness for you and absolutely nothing in return.* Maybe I was born on August 17, 1979, to come into your world and love you for twenty-two years and then begin to show you that life can be better. Life can be good!

Mom, I love you! Please don't be mad at me. I know it feels way weird for me to tell you this stuff, but I would say this to Jason, and I do tell him whenever I feel like I need to tell him something. So I thought, why shouldn't I be able to tell my own mom these things? I've prayed about this letter for six months now, and today God told me it was time. I just want to make things better for us!

Obviously, you will have to respond to this, and that will be hard. So you can do it however you feel most comfortable, but I just want you to know how much I love you and that I would never say any of this if I didn't believe with all my heart that it could make things better.

Love,
Suzanne

~

That was letter number *one*! Yeah, honesty is *not* easy and it's not a onetime thing. Eventually, it is healing, no matter how it is received. I would say that my relationship with my mom is about 95 percent different today than it was in October 2001. And I now see her in a completely different way than I ever could have imagined! Since that first door that I decided to kick open, there has been plenty of honesty from both sides of our relationship. I began to see the why in all of the things I just expected her to be able to change. She told me things that made everything make so much sense. There have been moments of joy and moments of awkwardness, but every moment of being honest with each other has done nothing but make us closer.

My mom is a fighter, she endures, she is strong, and she is passionate about love in so many ways. You don't take a woman like that and let the pain of her past continue to destroy her future if you can at all help it. *And you can*, by simply opening a door of honesty that, no matter what is said, will not ever be shut again. Forget how badly you just need a mom to be a mom. People can only give what they have, and at some point, if you have more strength than them, start giving back without focusing on what you wish you could receive. *When we focus on what we do not have, we overlook all that we do have!* God will always fill in the empty spaces while you are waiting for your wounds to heal. He's not a Band-Aid. He's more like Neosporin.

Did I say everything right? No, absolutely not! Did I say more than I needed to? Probably so. Did it work for our relationship? Yes—it worked because it was honesty!

You can teach people to listen to who you really are by refusing to be dishonest with them. If they are meant to be a part of your life, they will eventually listen. If they aren't meant to be a part of your life, they will distance themselves from you, and you will have to let them go. You can't make someone accept the real you, but you can *refuse* to give them the fake you. Either way, you are the only you there will ever be. So be you because God made you for a purpose!

seven

Finding Grace

My mom had a brother named David. He was one of the most handsome men I've ever seen. David's life, now, to me feels almost like a movie. I only saw him every once in a while, and every time he was around, I felt sick to my stomach because I never knew if he would have a place to sleep that night or food to eat when he left. After my grandma died, he pretty much ran away from home. He would come to church about two or three times a year, and I would pray the entire service for him to give his life back to Jesus and start *living*. I thought about him day and night. His life was so far from what I knew as a normal Christian life that I always believed he would go to Hell when he died if he didn't change everything about himself.

At the end of February 2002, he was in an accidental car wreck, and he did not make it. We all took it pretty hard, especially since this was also how his mom had died. None of us knew for sure where his heart was with God. The truth is that not everyone goes to Heaven when they die. The Bible is pretty clear that we can't just live whatever life we want to, and then expect to go to Heaven just because we are "good" people. But above our actions, God sees our hearts. Learning how to step out of the role of judge was very hard for me to do. Most of the people in my life had nothing but harsh opinions of others and their actions. Grace was something we sang about and prayed for after every bad thing we did, and every bad thought we had. Grace was not what we gave to people we disagreed with. This limited understanding of grace made it hard for me to see how God could save a sinner who couldn't seem to stop sinning. I had heard, all my life, that "your works are not what will get you to Heaven". Yet I was terrified that my mistakes would keep me from it.

A couple months before David died, he had been making efforts to be at church. Not that church is what saves a person, but because of this, we could see that he was having a change of heart and making an effort to turn his life around. I actually believe his heart was longing for God all along, but this time was different, and he had obviously been trying to get his life straightened out and on the right track. Seeing these steps he had been taking and the difference in his eyes was very encouraging for me, but I still feared that he had not made it to Heaven.

David had a lot of cards stacked against him. He chose to stack them up even higher, but God sent his son to die for us "while we were still sinners," and he knew that in our humanity we could never be perfect. *Jesus* is the one who made a way for us. Who are *we* to judge each other's hearts?

Oh, if I could go back and delete all the thoughts I had when I saw people walking down the street with more than one set of earrings, tattoos, shorts that were too short, drivers who cut me off, and rude grocery store workers who probably just needed a friend. It's embarrassing to think about the difference in the feelings I had toward these people vs. the feelings that Jesus had for them.

My father-in-law preached David's funeral, and I realize it won't mean as much if you don't know the trials of his life, but I wish the whole world could have been there. He talked about the prodigal son and how the Bible says, "While he was still far off, his father *ran* to him." I believe that God saw David coming his way while he was still "dirty and poor" on the outside (just like the prodigal son), still not all that we thought he should be but with his heart headed toward his father, and that his father *ran* to him in the moment he knew his son would receive him. To us, this meant that God saw David's desire to get where he had always longed to be, and allowed him to come to his eternal home, to see the face of the one who saved him, to finally be with his mom again, and to live in total peace for the first time ever. How's that for a whole new perspective on grace? God the Father did not see the messed up life that we saw. God the Father saw the *heart* of his son. I fully believe that people have to make Jesus Christ the lord of their life and turn from their ways that do not reflect him. I also believe that Jesus is the only way to Heaven, but what he means to each of our hearts, only we could ever know.

The morning of David's funeral, I was in the shower crying, begging God to give me total peace about his soul. Keep in mind that I had no idea what the message was going to be or where Papa was going to go with all of our uncertainty. God gave me this poem at that very moment. I was asked to read it at his funeral that same day.

~

March 2002

To my uncle David,

Although we are grieving
Inside and out,
We are also rejoicing
And praising God with a shout.

Though Satan thought he had you
And the rest of us too,
God has confirmed time and again
He's safely holding you.

Your soul is no longer our burden.
God has lifted the load
But when you've prayed for so long and loved so much,
It's really hard to let go.

We hear of all these people
And how you believed in them.
We only wish you had believed in yourself
The way that we all did.

Lie down and rest
Or jump up and run.
The choice is now yours;
You belong to the Son.

We love you and miss you
And can't believe you're gone,
But some day we will see you
And we know it won't be long.

We love you,
Your family

~

eight

Finding Patience

I had two main dreams in life: I wanted to marry Jason Dorsey and I wanted to be a mom. Looking back on the years of my life that I'm sharing with you in this book, it's pretty clear *now* why God wanted me to wait to have babies. But it does not change how badly my heart was hurting in those moments. I had been buying baby stuff since before I was married. I had so many things, years before I ever had a baby. I bought clothes, books, blankets, toys-—I loved babies and baby stuff. At this point we had been praying for a baby for about four years.

One day I went into the room I thought was going to be a nursery and sat in the middle of the floor and started crying. I cried so hard because a few days before that, I had dreamed that I had a baby. The nurse placed the baby in my arms. I looked down, but just before I could see the face of the miracle I had been waiting so long to see, I woke up. When I woke up, I honestly felt like someone had taken my baby away from me. To some, that may sound crazy, but to anyone who's ever wanted a baby for several years and had a vivid dream of what your baby would be like, I am certain that you understand. After I had no tears left and had used up all the tissues, I wrote this next poem.

~

July 2002

Already in My Heart

I am sitting in your room right now,
Listening to the silence that will soon be gone.

I wish you were here with me
But I know it won't be long.

I had a dream the other night
And I almost saw your face.

When I awoke, my heart broke.
How do I get back to that place?

I have many stories to tell you
And many memories to make.

We'll pray every night these words:
"The Lord my soul to take."

I wonder what your favorite book will be;
I have many you can choose from.

There's not much in your room right now
But that will change as soon as you come.

I know God has your birthday planned
And it will be the perfect day.

I just want to hold you and kiss you and sit here and smile:
That's what you'll hear me say.

For now, I will continue to wait,
As hard as it may be,

Because I know it will be worth it all
When you come home with me.

I loved you before I knew you.
I will love you once you're gone.

How can someone you've never met
Give your heart such a song?

~

While waiting for God to give me a baby, I was super blessed to be able to keep my cousin's baby boy. He was the sweetest, most loving little boy I'd ever been around. Anyone who was around him instantly wanted to take him home and keep him forever. His parents worked the second shift at the post office, so we actually got to have him every evening during the week. We got to eat dinner together, read books, watch *SpongeBob*, and even tuck him in at night because he would fall asleep before his parents came to get him. It was a great experience for Jason and me to kind of sort through how we would do things if we had our own child someday. It also made my impatience that much greater and made me want my own child more than anything in life. I also wrote this next poem during this time.

~

November 2002

Someday

When I see a child,
For a moment I dream:

What would it be like?
Heaven, it seems.

To wake up and see
The face of your own,

To tuck them in at night,
Knowing they'll never be alone...

I would tell them about Jesus
And we would sing of his love.

We could listen to the crickets call
And count the stars above.

I would hold them in my arms so tight
And read them stories every night.

Sometimes my dream does come true
But only for a moment in time

Because each child that visits here
Has to go home: they're not mine.

Is it wrong to wish sometimes they were
And that they'd never have to leave?

I just love kids, and when I see their faces,
My heart skips a beat, I believe.

I pray every day for God to make me a mother.
My child I would love more than any other.

It's hard to imagine exactly what I'd feel.
I guess someday I may find out if my dream ever becomes real.

Help me, God, to patiently wait.
Remind me that you're never late.

You know all, see all, hear all, and care.
Just promise me that you'll always be there

To take away this pain I feel
And assure me of your perfect will.

If all I ever do is dream, it's better than not feeling anything!
Thank you, God, for my dreams!

~

I knew that God was trying to teach me patience during this time of my life. Looking back, it seems as though he was also teaching it to my dad.

Earlier I told you a little about my dad. I told you that he hated his job but was determined to continue to do the right thing and provide for his family. My dad had been at this same company for about sixteen years, dealing every day with people he had no respect for and who had no respect for him or his God—all the while, sorting through his own doubts about his ability to trust God fully. These men would say things to him just because they knew it would get under his skin and set him off. He tried to explain God to them in the best way he knew but constantly felt like they were only causing him more questions instead of him causing them to believe.

One day, as I was praying for strength for him, I wrote this next poem. I wanted to take my dad's pain away so badly. That day, I was asking myself, "If I could have five minutes with these people who make my dad's life so stressful, what would I say to them?"

~

November 2002

You Can Believe

It's not enough to know He listens
If you've never heard him speak.

What kind of God is all around you
Yet distant from your needs?

You've tried to see him in the good times;
You've tried to trust him in the bad.

It seems like everyone around you
Has what you have never had.

Can't you feel God
In the wind that blows the trees?

And when you hear a baby laughing,
Does it not help you believe

That everything in this world
Could never compare to who he is?

And if you've ever seen a rainbow,
You can believe his promises.

You may think you've never seen him
Or felt his breath upon your face.

You may not believe he really loves you
Or even hears you when you pray.

Have you ever seen a sunset?
Heard the waves crash on the shore?

Seen the beauty of the autumn leaves
Or dreamed of something more?

Can't you feel God
In the wind the blows the trees?

When you hear a baby laughing,
Does it not help you believe

That everything in this world
Could never compare to who he is?

And if you've ever seen a rainbow,
You can believe his promises.
~

It always broke my heart to know that my dad was having a hard time at work. I had not yet learned to really love people without a critical heart. I felt like it was their job to listen and understand or keep their mouths shut. I was raised to believe "if you can't say something nice, you shouldn't say anything at all!" Though I'm not in full agreement with that rule now, it sure was how I lived my life and thought everyone else should too.

God started showing me, after I really began to listen, that even the people who *were* raised this way sometimes realize they have a right to feel the way they do...just like I did. Just because people don't always know how to express their pain in a pretty little box wrapped in grace and topped with a big fat bow of forgiveness doesn't mean we, as Christians, have the right see them as enemies—even if they are coming against us. What good will that ever be for them?

I knew God was trying to teach me what it really means to have patience for people I don't even like. God began to speak to me about how most people who hurt others do that because *they* are hurting inside. They don't realize that their pain is the cause of their unfiltered words to others. Their only coping mechanism is to make other people feel worse than they do. If we choose offense in those times when we could choose patience, we are only proving to these hurting people that they do have reason for believing God's love is conditional, instead of showing them what grace and healing look like. It's so hard to accept truth when the truth is that we are just as wrong as those who have wronged us. We must always remember that every soul matters to God, so every soul has to matter to us.

nine

Finding Understanding

All that I have told you so far should be enough to prepare you for this next poem. But I still want to explain for the sake of those in my family who will read this book. My family, just like yours, has opinions. There were times when these opinions affected the person I knew God had called me to be. I have a great family who loves me, stands up for me, and has also come a long way since the day I wrote this poem. Still, it was how I felt *at that time*, and I want you to see how being honest with your heart and sharing that with others is healing, even when it hurts.

I grew up hearing, and sometimes just knowing, these things being said of me: "You're just trying to be like Suzanne. Suzanne thinks she's better than everybody else. Don't mess with Ms. Holier-than-Thou. She doesn't even care about showing up for things that are important to us. She is so disrespectful." There were probably more along those lines, but these specific comments were the things that I dealt with in my heart while putting on a happy face and saying "I love you" as if the pain weren't there.

I didn't understand why doing the right thing made me wrong when it was what I'd been taught to do. Why was it offensive for people to want to be like me if I was doing the right thing? Following God's plan for my life sometimes took me away from my family's priorities. It wasn't that I chose to not be there; I was just trying to follow God—which was what I thought they wanted.

Some of the things they didn't see as sin, I did. I felt afraid to be myself around them for fear that I would come across as someone who had higher standards, making me even more of an alien in my own family. It was all very confusing for me.

Another uncle of mine, also a brother of my mom's, had always had a tight grip on my heart. I saw him as someone who was different from the rest of our family, kind of like I saw myself. One day, as he was leaving to go back to Texas, God gave me the words you are about to read.

I realized something that day that changed my life forever: I do not live to please my family. I live to please my God. When that finally reached the depths of my soul, a light came on and set me free. Until that point in my life, I couldn't figure out how to be like my family and at the same time stay focused on God's plan for my life. I wanted to either think and be like them or have them think and be like me. If this could happen, then they would accept me and I could stop worrying.

The day I wrote "What If I Understood," it finally came to me: if my uncle's life is the complete opposite of mine, and our family doesn't understand the way he thinks *or* the way I think, then why am I trying so hard to understand the way they think? I know they have said things they regret. So have I! I know they have said things they didn't mean, but whether or not they ever sit me down and say, "Suzanne, I just want you to know I understand now, and I'm sorry for whatever I said or even wanted to say that made you doubt that I'm proud to call you family," I can't let that affect the way I listen to and obey God's voice. It hurts to feel misunderstood, rejected, and alone, whether you are right or wrong. I thought, "If it hurts me this bad, it must really hurt my uncle too." I hoped that if I could show him that I understood him, then he might be able to understand me. That would at least be encouraging for us.

~
November 2002

What If I Understood?

I tried to keep from writing again
But when I saw the tears in your eyes,

I couldn't help but wonder:
Are they the same ones that are in mine?

Could it be we're not so different
Even though they say we are?

Do you feel my pain while I feel your shame
Even though we're miles apart?

They call you the stubborn outcast
And me "Ms. Holier-than -Thou."

Would they let me in if I were you,
Or you if to God you would bow?

Is it a sin to be the good one
And to not love anything bad?

Do you feel like even if you came back,
Not everyone would be glad?

How bad in their eyes is sin to God?
How far do you have to go?

How good in their eyes is way too holy?
How close to God is too close?

Is it wrong to see the world God made
And walk down roads he paves?

Do you wish someone would understand
And that your mind would let your heart lead the way?

Would you die for me? I know you would:
I see it when I look into your eyes.

Would I die for you? Yes, in a heartbeat,
If it could take away the lies.

In all my life I'd never understood
How people could live like you,

Never thinking maybe you don't understand
How people could live like I do.

If we could meet in the middle,
Would they see the perfect one?

Just a smoke here and drink there,
Working out our own salvation.

How do we make them understand?
How do we make them proud?

Being *me* or being *you*:
Either voice seems too loud.

I know you think that I'm the one
Who could never feel your pain

But if you cry, I'll see it, and if you love God, I'll believe it
And you'll never be alone again.

I'm not always holy
And you're not always lost.

That's why Jesus died: 'cause we could never pay
What it really costs.

Does it even matter
Who, what, why, or how

If in your heart and mine
We'd become whom God made us, and do it starting now?

I tried to keep my distance
But when you said good-bye,

I saw the tears in your eyes
And you saw the tears in mine.

P.S.
When no one else was there and we just couldn't get it quite right,
The grace of God protected our hearts from bitterness, day and
night.

There's a lot of pain in you, I know, and a lot of pain in me,
But the family God has placed us in loves us, unconditionally.

If we could say what we really feel and somehow let them know,
I bet we'd both be very surprised at the love they'd have to show.

~

In our lives we face giants that, without God, we will never
defeat. If we learn to see things through the eyes of God, we too
can find the good in everyone. The people that hurt us, either

intentionally or unintentionally, will be forgiven, possibly without us even realizing we have forgiven them. I believe, more every day, the pain inside of our hearts is only the pain we choose to not let go of.

God helped me to see that he could heal my hurt, when all along I was thinking the only way for healing was through apologies from those who had hurt me. I had no hope of that happening and therefore never looked for healing. *I just kept accepting pain.* Once I began to love the way God loves, unconditionally and without yesterday mattering, without expecting people around me to change and say, "I'm sorry," my healing process took off in a fast-forward motion.

I had always hoped to see a change but wasn't expecting it. I learned through emotional healing (the ministry I referred to earlier with Glenn Dorsey) that anything said of me that God wouldn't say doesn't matter. I honestly believe that! No longer did opinions, whether from family, friends, or enemies, affect me the way they had all my life. The things that offended me I began to see as simply pain in other people's hearts. How could their pain be of less value than me feeling good about myself? Just because people hurt me doesn't mean they wanted to. If they weren't trying to, how could that offend me? I can't fix the way they see me, but I can fix how that feels when it gets to my heart by forgiving them every single time. *That changed everything for me!*

God sees what we do and hears what we say, but he also knows what we mean. If peace is going to rule my heart, I must see people the same way God does. I can't always know what people mean, but I can choose to believe they don't mean something hurtful—especially if I know they love me. Who knows what happened to that little boy beside me in the fifth grade, the one who hated everybody and everything, the one who thought he was so cool but had the worst attitude, the one who called me "ugly" every day? He may be that new guy that walked into church this morning and sat down in front of me with tears streaming down his face because someone finally chose to see past his actions and believe that his heart mattered more.

November 2002 was a busy time for my heart. There were a whole lot of things God started dealing with me about, and I couldn't stop writing. The next thing I wrote was for my husband's grandpa. Grandpa Dorsey was a unique man who grew up in a world of pain. His dad was an alcoholic who would come home and destroy what little food had been prepared. The man would beat his wife in front of their kids, and the kids would go outside and sleep there, just to get away from him. In a very brave attempt to give her kids a normal life, Grandpa Dorsey's mother chose to keep all nine of her children, instead of letting family services put them in foster care. She raised them to love God and to forgive the people in their lives who hurt them. Several of those children grew up to be ministers, and all of them grew old serving God.

My husband is a third-generation preacher of the Bible who is living in the blessing of God, which has been passed down because his grandpa *chose* to forgive his own father, which allowed him to be the best father he could be. It's such a beautiful thing to see, and being there at Thanksgiving every year always feels like a victory service to me—a slap in Satan's face and one more year of watching the ongoing miracle of grace. One Thanksgiving Day, I went in the back room by myself and wrote these words:

~

November 2002

Like Grandpa

Another Thanksgiving as we sit with open ears,
Our bellies full, our eyelids drooping, but longing just to hear

What he has to tell us, even if we've heard it before.
He points his finger with tears in his eyes, saying, "Son, just keep loving God more!"

If the world stopped turning, what a perfect way to go as we're listening to his sweet voice,
To step into heaven on streets paved with gold and enter where angels rejoice.

Maybe we've just never seen such passion in another:
Could it be that he's the closest thing to Jesus we've discovered?

What will we do when the day arrives that his jokes will be no more?
Will we laugh when we remember him just like he was before?

Will we pick up the slack that will be left behind?
Stopping everyone we see, making sure they can find

The way to salvation we were called to share with them?
But we always found a way to leave it up to him

Because we knew he would tell them about Jesus with no shame
And if he'd say it, we wouldn't have to... why are we so weak, selfish, and lame?

He makes life seem so simple, never fearing tomorrow,
Only living for what Jesus does and learning from his sorrow.

He'll make you laugh, then make you cry,
Have you singing with angels and ready to fly,

Make you ready to live or ready to die—
But you'll never be ready to say good-bye.

How could we ever be like Grandpa?
A lifetime of faithfulness, I guess.

But I know if we could be even half of who he is,
God would see us as the best.

When I see your life, I can see my dreams fulfilled, and my heart
does sing.
If I ever stop to consider the cost, I'll remember that it's worth
everything!

I love you, Grandpa Dorsey!

~

ten

Finding Determination

Being an only child either gives you an intense desire to latch onto the people around you or makes you not want to be around anyone. For me as a child, it was the first one. I had a very close relationship with my cousins, and particularly three brothers who were third cousins to me (but felt more like my brothers). This family was your perfect church attendance, always dressed up and hair fixed, Sunday dinner with the family, Sunday school teachers for years and years—that kind of family. My family spent so much time with them. When I was really small, we lived right across the street from each other. No matter where we moved after that, it was a normal, everyday thing to see them for a certain reason or for no reason at all.

The middle son was my age. One day when we were in eighth grade, I came home to find out that their parents were getting divorced. Of course, there were years of pain on both sides that I had no idea was there, so I was completely in shock. But my shock meant nothing compared to the shock that these three brothers had that day. What happened after that is not my story to tell but one can imagine (considering the obvious effects that divorce brings to a family with 3 children). Skipping ahead ten years to the time I wrote this next poem, I was married and had moved back to my hometown, where I was trying my best to help restore that family.

Not once in the last ten years or for the next ten would there be a day that every member of that family did not cross my mind and my heart. At this point, the youngest son was trying his hardest to bring his mom back to Jesus, and my heart was aching for him. I wanted so badly to see him have the desires of his heart and the dreams he had now—what *used* to be known as his normal, stable, everyday way of life. People live this way every day, wondering if ever they will feel again what they thought they would always have. It just kills me!

~

February 2003

It Was Only for a While

A little boy comes in smiling
Because his day was extra good.
He opened up his lunchbox
And there was more than just his food.

His mom had given him a special note:
"You Are My Shining Star!"
And though the teacher made him work,
He knew that home was not that far.

The next day he was so upset.
He said some bullies had gotten him wet,
Pushed him down in the mud
And called him a name,
Spit in his face and said, "No, you can't play!"

He thought his life was over.
He wouldn't make it another day.

He thought he'd never have another friend...
Then he heard his "momma" say:

This is only for a while.
Listen to me, my sweet child.
If you'll find the strength to pray,
Jesus will take your pain away.

I know you want to cry.
If you do it's all right.
Now, let me see that smile.
This is only for a while.

Many years had passed, and the boy got much older.
With all the strength that was within him,
He grew up fast, maybe because he had to,
But the bond was still between them.

People often wonder
How the boy so deeply loves her.
When he looks back on the past,
He sees only beauty in his mother.

His mother tries to be stronger
Than she often really is,
Taking all that she has lost,
Believing she really does deserve this.

When she lays her head on her pillow each night,
No one ever sees the pain
Because she tells them everything's all right
And herself is whom she blames.

Each time the boy looks at his mother,
He hears the words she used to say

And wonders if she has forgotten
How to take lemons and make lemonade.

The boy knows what he should do
But doesn't want to go alone.
It's just so hard to do what's right
When his mother is sitting at home.

He wishes the words she once shared with him
Could make a difference in her life today.
He hates to see her tear stained eyes
And really wants to say:

Was it only for a while?
Was it only for your child?
Did you hear yourself say pray?
He'll take your pain away.

What about those times I cried?
You always said it was all right.
Did you hear yourself say smile?
Was it only for a while?

Someday soon he'll be a man,
Won't always be around to say,
"Mom, I know you still love Jesus,
But can he have your heart today?"

~

It turns out she hadn't forgotten how to make lemonade. About ten years after I wrote this, the boy's mom came back to Jesus, and she has now spoken in different places about drug awareness and serves God to help restore broken, addicted families. "The boy" is on the mend, and I am still praying for total healing in this entire family.

Some people you just have to believe in. For me, it's them! You can't convince me that there's no hope. When you see a family at the bottom of the bottom and watch God raise them up, there is no point in saying, "what if"—it's only "wait and see!"

Does God let people go through the fire and then use that to reach other people? I totally believe the answer is yes. Is it God's will for you to hurt? I believe the answer is no. God did not create us for pain. He created us for relationship. But because we are human and we live with other humans, we are going to mess up and cause pain in each other. I don't believe it is God's will for you to *be* hurt but I do believe it is God's will for you to take your scars and show others how they can make it too. God sent his only son to die on a cross for us because that's what it took. He knows what it takes to reach us. Sometimes it may take pain for us to believe that he is the healer. God did not place us in an impossible world of sin to sit back and watch us suffer. He gave us a way to get back up every time we fall and unconditional love for our hearts to feel along the way. Your life could possibly be the doorway to another person's freedom. If you were meant to be strong for someone else to have hope, then your trials are on the way, but *your victories will be enough.* Just keep following Jesus and be who you really are, scars and all. People who have pain want to talk to someone who understands what they've been through. To them, your scars are their hope.

Craig Groeschel said, "We might impress people with our strengths, but we connect with people through our weaknesses." T. D. Jakes said, "God will never anoint who you pretend to be—he will only anoint who you are." I agree with both of these statements. For those of you in ministry, whether you are in full-time ministry or not, you have to remember that people *only* need you to be who you are. If you aren't being yourself because you think people will be turned off by the real you, they will still be turned off because they will know you aren't being yourself. Chances are, even when you fail, people will want to follow you if you are *always* honest about the person you really are inside. We don't trust people because they do not fail. We trust people because they admit it when they do.

In April 2003, I was having a hard time with all of this "be yourself" stuff. We were the youth pastors at our home church in Beebe, Arkansas, and some of the kids were pretty vocal about how they were not going to listen to me. I also felt a lot of pressure because this was my family's church. Though I felt much more support at this time than in previous years, I was still very concerned about the way I handled myself. I wanted to act grown up—because I was— but I also felt like people would think I was trying to be something I was not. Most days, God helped me to remember that the only affirmation I needed would come from him. On this particular day, I was struggling with many things, like how to be honest but gracious at the same time, how to deal with people that didn't like me, and how to keep on "shining for Jesus" when what I really wanted to do was crawl in a hole and be by myself.
~
April 2003

Help Me

God, help me not to ever be myself
Until I become just like you.
It's just so hard to not say what I know,
To be honest, straightforward, and true.

Sometimes *I* win, and not the woman
I know you have made me to be.
I know it's wrong but I get so mad
And loud comes out, you see.

Can I ever be right when somebody's watching?
Can I ever just be me?
Can I ever say what's in my heart?
Can I ever just feel free?

Someone's always looking
To see if I'm going to be right.
And what if I'm wrong? What does that mean?
Can they no longer see my "light"?

I smile when I'm happy,
And when I'm sad, I do pout.
When I try to make a point, I usually end up not knowing
What even I myself am talking about.

Everyone sees right through me.
Is this really the road I should take?
How can I be the person they need
Making mistake after mistake after mistake?

I know I'm only human
And you're strong when I am weak
But can I have one day
With no one judging me every time I speak?

I'm not asking for a different life.
You know I love my own.
I love my husband, my family, my friends,
My church, my house, and my home.

I just want to be me sometimes, you see,
And know that it's OK to.
God, help them to see what my heart really means
While I'm trying to become more like you.
~

eleven

Finding Inspiration

While my dream of having kids had not yet come true, my dream of being Jason's wife was everything and more than I could have ever imagined. Jason is the person who taught me how to think in a healthy way. He taught me communication. He taught me how to live an honest life and not settle for anything else. He showed me the difference in saying "I love you" and putting every ounce of effort you have into causing someone to *want* to love you—even those who would've loved you anyway. Jason is the place I go for answers, love, strength, approval, honesty, peace, quiet, understanding—the place I can dump my heart out where it's never held against me.

When I say that I have the best there is, I honestly believe that. He is not perfect. He is stubborn and he is extremely hard to keep up with, but he is the reason I have the courage to even write this book. He taught me how to obey God and put everyone else's thoughts and opinions on the back burner if they do not line up with God's plan. He taught me how to deal with fear. He taught me how to live victoriously. He taught me how to do the right thing, even when it hurts.

While he was teaching me these vital life lessons, I was going through the fire of figuring out my place in life, in ministry, as an adult daughter, as a wife, as a young woman who thought she might never be able to have kids. I was also the daughter-in-law of the man who was my own pastor, my biggest intimidator, the one with the godly wisdom that I always believed in, the man I would never want to let down *and* the boss of my husband. I was in a place where I was a member of the largest family in the church. This was the place where everyone knew I was not raised in ministry, and where I had also been viewed as a clueless person most of my life.

You name it: I felt it! I depended on Jason's every move, word, and choice. I would cry like a baby almost every time he walked out the door. I didn't want to be without him for one second. I can't believe God gave him not only the patience to deal with me in the right way but the heart to stay completely in love with me, all at the same time.

At this time, it was no longer that I was afraid to be alone. I just felt so strong when he was with me (which was a really great new feeling) that being without him made me doubt everything about myself.

One day after he left to go to work (about seventy-five feet away from our house, because we lived in the church parking lot), I wrote "The Love of My Life."

~

April 2003

The Love of My Life

He is running through the house, but for a moment he pauses: "Do I look OK? Thank you for my egg sandwich! I'll see you at lunch. I love you!" As he walks out the door, a tear comes to my eye. In my head I know I'll see him in just a few hours, but all my heart knows is he's gone. I can tell it everything's going to be fine and calm the darts that pierce it, but when I watch *A Wedding Story*, the tears again will come. He literally makes my heart skip a beat every time he looks my way.

Negative blood doesn't run through his body. He doesn't understand the point. I guess that's why he thinks I can do anything. If I had known the man he would someday be when I married him five years ago, I could have never gone through with it because he deserves so much more than me. Sometimes he makes me mad, but he is usually right, and so my anger dissolves quickly.

When I watch the way he does his work, I want the whole world to see him. Nobody knows him like I do or could ever appreciate his dedication to everyone who asks for it and even those who don't. His motto is "If you see something that needs to be done, do it!"

Have you ever looked at somebody and felt strength leaping from them to you? Have you ever almost broken your teeth from gritting them together so hard as you were hugging someone tight? Have you ever been unable to sleep at night for fear that this could be the last time you may ever get to hold this person? This is how he makes me feel.

Nobody could love me like he does. Nobody could motivate me like he does. He's my hero, my best friend, and the love of my life. He makes me see things I can't see for myself. He makes the stars in my world brighter and the load of my life lighter, and even though when I look in the mirror, beauty is not what I see, when he looks at me, I feel beautiful!

I love you, Jason Thomas Dorsey, and *you* are the reason I even know what that means.

~

It's so amazing what happens in your heart when you aren't living every moment in fear that your true feelings may be revealed. As you begin to be honest with yourself and the people around you in a way that you never have been before, but in a respectful way, it not only changes the way you see people, but it also changes the way you *think* they see you. Because I now completely understood how it was possible to love someone unconditionally and feel the same in return, I was determined to feel that for the people closest to me and find inspiration in the places it had always been, that my heart just couldn't see before.

As you read earlier in the book, I had a very hard time expressing myself to my mom. We can live 24-7 with people, feel total trust that they will always be there for us, see them invest their entire life into making us happy, and still hold bitter feelings toward them.

I think that my mom is probably the person I'm the absolute hardest on with my expectations, and possibly the one person I am the most adamant about protecting. Yes, my mother said things like, "You are the only person who loves me, you are my only happiness, I can't make it without you," and on and on. Hearing those things sparked a huge conflict in my heart that I didn't even realize was happening. I felt very loved and appreciated, like I had something to offer, like I was super special and could make her smile at the drop of a hat. I also felt trapped, sad, mad, and guilty for having any kind of life that didn't involve her.

In my mom's defense (which is my superhero side job), my mom was eighteen years old when she had me and chose to marry my dad – knowing there'd be no shortage of issues between them.

Then my mom lost her mom when I was one. She lost her best friend, the parent she was most like, her support system, and the person who was going to completely spoil her kid rotten...and did I mention? It was her *mom!* With so many things against her, and not really knowing much about healthy two-way communication at this point in her life, she did what anyone would do: She survived. She tried. She gave her pain to God and then went back and picked it up, over and over again. She failed. She won. She was happy. She was sad. She threw herself into the only thing she knew was unconditional for her—me.

I can't tell you if my ability to communicate was squashed out of me by her inability to let go of her control, if it was simply that I grew up in a home where everything that was said was a possible argument starter and honesty only meant pain, or if it's because I truly am not meant to speak with my mouth so that God can use me to speak through my heart. Whether it was one of those, all of those, or none of those, God showed me that my job was to stop blaming anyone or anything for what I kept claiming I could not do. As long as I was blaming other people for what I couldn't be or do (even if that just meant being happy), I was refusing God the room to show me that I could.

He also showed me that though my mom still had a lot of pain inside her heart, causing her reactions to hurt me, I had to begin to see the *greatness* inside of her. He said, "I made your mom! I know the pain and the guilt that she faces every day. I also made you. Not one moment have I left your side, and not one moment have I left hers. You aren't responsible for fixing her. You cannot change her. You can love her without being hurt by what you cannot change, if you will realize she is human just like you. The heart inside of a mother loves uncontrollably, recklessly, passionately, sometimes painfully, but always unconditionally. You love who she is, and I will work on who she is not!"

I told God I would do that from then on. That next Mother's Day was unlike any previous ones. My sweet words to her weren't followed by an unspoken "if only I could fix this." It was the first time I had written to my mom from my honest heart, and I loved everything that my heart had to say!

~

May 2003

The Greatest One Yet

Your dreams were not to see the world
Or be Miss Universe.
You didn't ask to hold the stars
Or even a flashy expensive purse.

You never really cared
About having a big career.
You simply wanted to be a mom
And always have me near.

You woke up and were happy
When you could've chosen to cry.
You could have hung your head in pointless shame
But you looked up to the sky.

You could've listened to what people said
They knew you'd never be
But you always said "I thank you, God,
For giving me my dreams."

Because of who you are
And always were to me,
Of all the dreams I've ever had,
There's one that supersedes:

To love my child and make it known
The way that you love me.
To be the best *mom* in the world:
That's what I long to be.

You have taught me so much,
Things I'll never forget,
But not to love this world
Is the greatest one yet.

I try to be thankful
And at the end of every day.
Whether I am happy or sad,
In my heart I hear you say:

"You can work hard to build a mansion
That may be destroyed in a day.
You can work hard to build a family
That death may take away.

You can wait for all the fantasies
But they may never come true.
You can reach high to climb a mountain
But someone might outreach you.

Then you can wake up and be happy
Or you can choose to cry.
You can hang your head in pointless shame
Or look up to the sky.

You can listen to what people say
They know you'll never be
Or you can always say, 'I thank you, God,
For giving me my dreams.'"

Thank you, Mom, for teaching me that life is not
about this world! I love you!

~

twelve

Finding Love

The most life-changing quote I think I've ever read, one that I use over and over again, is one I saw hanging in the bathroom of our first pastor's home once we began full-time ministry. I believe it was no coincidence. Because of the effect it had on me, I still wonder if it was hanging there for me alone! It said, "God grant me the serenity to accept the people I cannot change, the courage to change the one I can, and the wisdom to know it's me. —Unknown."

It sounded so good, and I knew God was speaking to me in that moment, but I hadn't learned how to change *me*, and so I held on to that for a while before God started showing me the true meaning of it. Once I started really noticing the changes happening in me, I remembered that quote from three years prior. I began to look back and see this extremely difficult journey I was on as healing. It was obvious that the more I opened up and let go of my pain, the more God was filling me with his perfect love. I fell madly in love with *love*!

I then knew what it meant. I understood its ways. I began to see how it conquers all. It became my passion! I was addicted. I found love in every hiding spot it had been placed. I was beginning to see how love was very different from guilt and that the two combined could never accomplish anything. Even when I saw every reason to not believe in a person, the fact that my heart was changing so much gave me faith to believe that *any* heart could heal. I became very sappy, and because my heart was becoming empty of fear and pain, I was able to see *love* in every moment. I believed in it! I believed in the power behind it! I believed it would work for everyone I knew!

In June 2003, my very young cousin, who had recently been a student in our youth group, was getting married. Ignoring people's opinions and what they just didn't understand about love, my cousin chose to listen to her heart and marry the man she didn't know how to *not* love! I could relate. The night before her wedding, I wrote this poem for her and her soon-to-be husband.

~

June 2003

Because of Who We Are Together

Because of who we are together
We can never be apart.
Your love is my tomorrow
And my home is in your heart.

When I see your face, it calms me
And I know I'll be OK.
Without you there's no future:
I would not last a day.

I see you in the morning
And my heart begins to beat.
I know you're right beside me
But I never want to sleep.

We are what people dream of
But never take the chance.

They're scared of what may happen
Or that time may end their dance.

You are the missing piece
That I never thought I'd find.
They tell me of regrets I'll have.
Maybe so...you're still mine.

What more could a person ask for?
What more could they possibly dream?
You've given me the stars to hold—
Nothing better could there be.

As time goes by, our love will grow
Into one heart that beats forever
And we can never be apart
Because of who we are together.

~

My cousin has been married for eleven years now. She and her husband have three children, and they love and live for God probably more than any family I know! I am more than proud! I am humbled to be a part of their family. I look up to them and want to be like them. If God says, "Go," then it's OK to trust him without knowing the future, and it's OK to trust him with other voices telling you you're crazy. There is so much freedom in serving Jesus no matter what or who comes against you. This family is and forever will be an example of that kind of freedom!

Love can give rise to the best feelings in the world, and love can give rise to the worst. You may have heard the saying, "God may ask you to do something you don't want to do, but he will never ask you to do something you regret." At this time in our lives, God was asking us to become missionaries with Youth Alive for the state of

Arkansas. One of the hardest days of my life was telling the students at Beebe First Assembly that we were leaving.

Things were going so well, and we had developed such a connection with those kids. We had friends! We had things figured out! We were just as surprised as the church was when God asked us to leave, and I wrote this for my kids—the ones God gave me while I was waiting for my own.

~

July 2003

Dear RPM,

I look at your faces with some eyes crying,
Others confused, and some even mad.
You can't understand and wish you were dreaming.
I know 'cause I've been there: It hurts really bad.

You may think it's easy, exciting, and fun
For us to be leaving—another race to be won.
And here you're left feeling like there's no one to trust
Or tell you, "You can, you will, and you must."

But what if we told you to listen to God's voice
And then we, because it was too hard, didn't make the right choice?

Two years ago I came here not knowing what to expect
And a big wall was between us I could easily detect.
But that wall started to crumble after some pain grief and strife,
And to me now you're beautiful: You're my kids. You're my life.

I can't say that I understand
Everything God is doing

But I owe it to you
To go where he's leading

Because that's what I want you to do.

I have hollered and cried and begged and pleaded.
At times you have wanted to give up and leave it.
But you didn't. I see you're not here just for me
And now my greatest joy comes in saying, "Satan, you're defeated."

Sometimes when I look back at my life
And think how things could have been different,
I'm always happy knowing that they weren't
And for a while you are what my life meant.

I know you'll be fine...
Some may even be happy,
But there's always that day when it's all said and done
And everyone has to get sappy.

We'll say our good-byes and start to drive away,
But as we look back, we hope this is what we'll hear you say:

"Jason and Suzanne? Yeah, they weren't all that bad.
Even though they made us do push-ups, I'm glad!

'Cause it made us stronger. Of course, not for Russell...
Well, he already had those great big muscles!

But yeah, we needed to have a few lessons.
I guess we learned a little in our Team Player sessions.

What about that time when Bro. Jason said he loved us?
You think he meant that? Well, he was a lot like Jesus.

We gave him so much attitude and complained about things that
meant nothing,
But I'm sure he knew we loved him and thought he was really
something!

They did tell us the truth, even though we already knew it.
I guess that's what they're good for, 'cause sometimes we really
blew it.

Well, I wonder who's coming in next.
I don't know what to expect,
But I'm sure God knows what we need and what we want,
'Cause after all, he's brought us this far and he'll be there for the
rest.

Man, I'm sure going to miss them
And I know they'll be missin' me,
'Cause how else, without a youth group,
Can their house ever get TP'd?"

Here's my heart, in a few more lines.
I hope you'll never forget it
Because what I say is what I mean,
So listen close to this last little bit:

If I hear that you're slipping
Or your hope is fading fast,
I can't promise you that you won't receive
A little visit from your past.

I know you won't let that be true,
Or ever let that happen
Because you're *my* kids,
And with Jesus there's no way you could be lackin'.

My greatest reward is in knowing you're determined
And you won't let Satan steal your *shout*.
When you think about us and our time spent together
I hope you'll be smiling from the inside out.

I love you with all of my heart!
-Suzanne

~

As you can tell, my heart had taken a huge turn at this point in my life. I was feeling stronger and very confident that God was making sense of my life. I felt like God was using me to reach out to people with unconditional love, instead of me using my own human efforts, which only left me feeling discouraged. I really did begin to see people like God saw them. I still didn't feel like I had much to offer, but I felt like it was OK to admit that. I felt like people would accept my honest love and that, for my purpose at this time, would be enough. I finally felt like life was a gift that God had given me instead of a war that I was forced to face. I felt loved, needed, appreciated, and hopeful!

We began this journey as missionaries in October 2003 and moved to Cabot, Arkansas, to begin raising our support. I felt honored to be a missionary. I felt honored to be the wife and best friend of a man that no one on earth could top. I felt honored to be the daughter of such amazing parents who were known for their battles but recognized for their victories! I felt total peace in God, whom I'd finally surrendered my life *and* my heart to.

Even though I still had a deep desire to be a mommy, I felt *whole* for the first time in my life. It was amazing just to be able to see a glimpse of where God was taking me and how far he had brought me. Can you believe what happened next?

thirteen

Finding Hope

~

December 2003

My "Now" Met God's "Now"

I have prayed, cried, dreamed, and *begged* for a baby for years
now. I've reminded God of his promises to me and been frustrated
because I couldn't stand the waiting. Knowing all along that God
was in control of my life, I've lost faith at times to believe in what
I knew was truth. I've been to so many altars and spent so many
days on my knees with tears streaming down my face, wondering
why all the people in my life, everyone but me, had a beautiful child
to call their own. I've watched and heard as mothers screamed at
their children in parking lots, saying, "Ugh, I just wish you would
shut up! Why can't you do anything right? What's wrong with
you?" I would always leave with a broken heart because I couldn't
take the children home with me. I've heard it said this way before:
"She's a mother with no children."
I can't begin to tell you how it feels to love someone that doesn't
exist. Once, I wrote these words: "I loved you before I knew you.
I will love you once you're gone. How can someone you've never
met give your heart such a song?" She kept me dreaming for what
I knew I'd someday have. She made me long to be a better person
so that when she came, she would have a mother she could be
proud of. She drove me to be disciplined in financial decisions

that would determine not only my future but also hers. She made my heart pound with excitement and hope. She made me listen to advice that I may not have otherwise cared about. She was beautiful to me, and even though some may have called it my fairy-tale world, I knew it was my future.

I woke up in Branson, with snow falling to the ground, on my six-year wedding anniversary and decided to take that test just one more time. I waited for what seemed like days. Three minutes... nothing. Ten minutes...nothing. Fifteen minutes had passed, and I was ready to throw it away. Jason said, "Just wait!" This was a word I had heard too many times before. About five minutes later, I went back to check one last time, and *there it was*: the faintest purple line I had ever seen. I held it up to the light and looked, hoping I was not imagining things. I said, "Jason, I think that's a line, but maybe I'm just wanting so badly to see it that I'm imagining it. What do you think?" He said, "It looks like a line to me. Take the other test!"

I took the next test. Here we go again, waiting, waiting, waiting, and then: "What in the world is that?" The entire window turned purple. Ugh...not the time for a defective testing stick! We immediately got in the car and headed to our friends' house in Springfield. As soon as we got into town, Jason went and bought two more tests. With each one, the line got darker and darker. I couldn't get into a clinic there (it was Saturday), so I had to wait until Monday to take a blood test. I would not be convinced until a doctor said, "Yes, it's positive! *You are pregnant!*" Tuesday morning (yes, you used to have to wait an entire day to get the results of a pregnancy test from the doctor's office), I got the call that I had waited five and a half years for: "Congratulations, Suzanne! *You are pregnant!*"

December 13, 2003, is the day that my "now" met God's "now." Isn't it funny how we think we know what we need and when we need it, but when it happens in God's timing, we always see how his timing makes much more sense than ours? When God says yes to the desires of our heart, then we get all excited, thinking he is also saying yes to our timing. The phrase "when my 'now' met God's 'now,'" which I'd heard preached about before, had never meant so much to me as on the day I heard I was finally going to be a mommy. God's timing actually coincided with mine and up to this point, besides my wedding day, it was the most wonderful day of my life! Thank you, Jesus!

~

I honestly believe that God had to begin my healing process before he could trust me with my own child. God knew me! He knew the expectations I had placed on my parents and that I would only place higher ones on myself. If I could not learn how to be open and honest with my parents and those around me, I would never be able to sort through the reality of being a parent myself. Knowing the pain and fear I had always dealt with, God wanted to show me that trials are not forever; they are temporary. Family is not perfect; it is unconditional. Failure is not measured by what you did not achieve; it is only measured by your loss of hope.

I began thanking God for my life. I started seeing my family as the *rock* that has made me who I am. I still hate the fighting, the pride, the lack of communication, and the bitter feelings that no one wants to talk about. I don't understand how people who love so intensely can hold back what they feel for those around them and think it makes a man weak to admit what he feels. It still drives me crazy to walk into a room and feel the heaviness of years and years of unspoken truths that are all covered up by "Happy Birthday! Merry Christmas! Happy Mother's Day!" I hate that I was raised, not just by my parents, but also by almost everyone around me, to be offended at the drop of a hat. But not for one second do I want to go back and take away the things I have learned. And not for one second do I believe that's who any of us really *want* to be. That one simple sentence keeps my heart from bitterness, and I just continue believing in the people I know they really are inside.

My family *was* the rock that was too heavy for me to hold up but was always strong enough to hold me up. It *was* the rock that never felt good when blocking me but was always there to defend me. It often felt like my biggest stumbling block but gave me higher ground to be able to see my purpose. Without offense, how do we learn grace? Without awkward moments, how do we learn confidence? Without moments of unnecessary rage, how do we learn self-control? Without pain, how do we learn forgiveness?

Being willing to let my heart be honest and say the things that had hurt me was slowly giving me the keys to forgiveness. It was opening my eyes to the reasons why people were the way they were. It didn't change what was happening around me; it changed what was happening inside of me.

Once my perspective on the things I'd been through changed, I never looked at people the same. When they would say something I didn't agree with or act a certain way that used to upset me for days, I would just forgive them. I saw past the words and asked God to show me their hearts—not just once but every single time. I let go of the desire for those around me to understand what I needed, realizing that God would provide that in his own special way. I simply loved the people around me for whom they were, and honestly left their intentions to be defined by God. This brought so much freedom to my heart.

After that, I honestly looked for affirmation from one place...OK, maybe two, but Jason is just so good at it. God is my main source of affirmation, and I want that more than anything. It's not so I can feel good about myself—it's so I can have enough courage to help others see their way to freedom. If God had a plan for me to reach hurting people, I could have never done that without understanding hurt. I was also so excited to throw all of this in Satan's face and say three words: "You lost, sucker!" My ability to see God work all of these things for the good was confirmation for my heart that Satan couldn't even claim the *pain* he had caused my family and me. Now you may not be a very emotional person, but I am, and every time I read that previous sentence, it makes me want to cry, shout, jump, and fall down on my knees, all at the same time. It's pretty exciting that simply believing God can work your pain for your good takes all of Satan's efforts to destroy you and demolishes them! Your only job is to *believe* that, and you will see it happen as well.

The next month was my parents' twenty-fifth wedding anniversary. Just saying that fills my heart with joy that only I could understand! I, being an only child, got to decide anything and everything about the party! We decorated the church with balloons and candles. We had yummy food, cake, punch, and many gifts. We invited everyone who had ever known them. Even several people I didn't expect showed up. After all, who wouldn't want to come celebrate twenty-five years of defeated doubt? I was thrilled to get to write three different things for that night, and I'm going to share two of them with you. The third was a message in a bottle for their eyes only.

~

January 2004

Someone like You

What kind of love can last
Through what seems like deadly winds,
Through the toughest times
And biggest mistakes
And childhood dreams that are shattered?

What kind of heart can be restored
After being broken into a million pieces,
After beating so strong with the excitement of a new life
And being stopped in an instant by a death so unexpected?

What kind of tears can be stopped
Flowing because of loneliness
And fear and rejection,
Because of freedom that was taken
And words that were said never meant
But still spoken and heard?

What kind of hope keeps you dreaming
For the joy that comes tomorrow
When today is covered by clouds,
When what once was your joy has now been taken
And you're left with a void no one can fill?

What kind of faith can carry you
From a place of darkness to light
Without saying a word,
Just by looking into eyes of forgiveness
And being held by the arms of love
That once only held rage?

It was said by G.W.C. Thomas,
"There is no greater love than the love that holds on
Where there seems nothing to hold on to."

Things are not always as they appear.
Love is not taken when life is.
Dreams are not shattered from a few bad days.
Time is not wasted while learning from mistakes.

So what kind of heart can cry and break and bleed
But dream and hope and believe
With faith and love and joy?

The kind of heart that is given by God
That says, "I will," and does,
That loves because it chooses to
And doesn't believe in giving up.

What makes life worth living
And chances worth taking?
What makes time worth spending
And tears worth crying?

Loving someone like you,
Someone who loves me too,
Someone who laughs when I'm happy
And cries when I'm sad
And wishes for me everything I've never had.

Your smile calms my fears
And your heartbeat gives me life.
Your presence makes me stronger
And your beauty makes me feel beautiful.

You are the love of my life,
You are the sparkle in my eye,
You are the one who knows me inside out,
You're the one who was there,
You're the one who held me.

~

January 2004

What a Journey

Today I'll be your hero
If you'll be my biggest fan.

Tomorrow I'll walk with you
If you'll take me by the hand.

Today I'll listen closely
If you'll tell me what you need.

Tomorrow I'll be stronger
Because today you trusted me.

Today I'll cry,
Only because that's what women do.

Tomorrow you can go and play
Because men need time too.

Today you will make my jaws flex and my nostrils flare,
And my voice will get too loud.

Tomorrow you will give me that smile
And I'll forget what I was talking about.

Today there'll be no money
And I'll work harder to make ends meet.

Tomorrow will be better
And you'll say, "Can we please go out to eat?"

There's not a lot we haven't heard
Or seen or done or felt

And what a journey this has been.
What an adventure we've been dealt.

I could've never made it the last twenty-five years
Of my life without you—no, never—

And I promise to give you what's left of my days
And my heart, forever and ever.

I love you, Mom and Dad! You are my heroes! Nothing and no one will ever convince me that I should have had it better. I hate what Satan used against us to keep us down, but I love watching God rip that to shreds and restore what only he can! I wasn't made because of you two; I was made so there would be a *"You two"*! God knew that without each other, as hard as that is to figure out, neither of you would make it. I got to be the glue, but you are the heroes.

What better life could a person have than to witness daily victory like we did? God loved you both so much that he created an entire person, in the middle of Satan's sinful and deceiving tricks, to give love to two people that otherwise may not have found it. And then he said, "You know what? I think I'll take that person that I created just to prove you wrong, Satan, and give her the most blessed life possible!" That's just my take, but *honestly,* that's the way I see it all. And it's so beautiful to watch God take all things and work them together for the good of those who love him and are called according to *his* purpose! No one else can do that and no one can destroy that!

Love,
Suzanne

~

fourteen

Finding Appreciation

Two things were happening in me at this point in my life, and both of them enhanced each other. I had a life growing inside of me, causing me to feel emotions I had never had before, and God was gluing my heart back together, leaving no room for bitterness to seep through the cracks. The two things happening on the inside of me were more confirmation that God currently had my life in the palm of his hand and always had since the day I was conceived. God knows my every step. He is the one who orders my steps, even though I don't always understand them.

One thing I never understood was why God allowed my grandma, my mom's mom, to die. It seemed so wrong. How could tearing apart a family like that be God's plan, and if it wasn't his plan, then why didn't he prevent it? For years, that's how I saw it. I never knew my MawMaw Teddene, but it feels like I did. I am told that she was the most amazing, beautiful, Christian woman anyone around her knew. I can't help but wonder what differences there would have been if she had not died that day.

Maybe I would've gotten to spend the night with her and make cookies. Maybe I could've talked to her about people that hurt me. Maybe I could've made her proud, and she would have come to see me at school plays and choir performances. Maybe she would have taken me shopping and wasted her money on me.

The thing I think about most is this: What if she could have understood me? Maybe she wouldn't have cared about my hair and clothes and attitude and mouthy ways. Maybe she would have looked past that and into my eyes, where it mattered. Maybe she would have asked to see my report cards and been OK with my Cs, because grandmas are proud of every*thing,* right? Maybe in the middle of the many family fights I heard, I could have run to her and covered my ears and let her *tell* everyone to stop. I bet they would have listened to her. I just didn't know. It made no sense to me. What I did know was that she *couldn't do* that for me, and more importantly, she couldn't do that for her own daughter. My mom was nineteen years old when she lost her mom.

Previously, Mother's Day meant sorrow, sadness, visits to the cemetery, and extreme efforts to give something to my mom that would bring her a few minutes of happiness on this dreaded day. Honest moment number 5,483,672: *I hated Mother's Day!*

It wasn't me who lost my mom. Why was I forced to be sad on this day? My mom and her brothers weren't trying to make me, or anyone else, feel that way, but because of the overwhelming sense of "this day is about the one thing we've all lost" *instead of* "this day is about the restoration we've all had" (mostly because they hadn't had it)...well, sadness kind of took over.

Although those were my honest feelings for many years, I still loved my mom intensely and always wanted the best for her on this day. The reality of how difficult it must have been for her was finally sinking into my brain and my heart. The reality was that moving on and becoming a strong, balanced person after losing your own mother, your best friend, the one who "gets" you whom you can never, ever get back or replace, at such a difficult time in your life, with a new baby and so many day-to-day struggles already, all while trying to live a godly righteous lifestyle and not really knowing how to communicate with your own father, or brothers, or even your own husband, can kind of make a person feel crazy.

God showed me that *time* does not heal a heart. It didn't matter how long it had been since my mom had gone through these trials. People can spend fifty years of their life trying to feel better. The only thing that can change your heart is admitting what's in there, releasing it, and letting God fill it back up with healing. I could not give my mom the joy she needed, no matter how hard I tried. I also could not expect her to get over these hurts just because they were in the past. What I felt like my mom needed was a place to simply be honest. This is one of the main reasons I finally started seeing my mom differently. This year for Mother's Day, I had a different wish for her. I wasn't searching for the perfect gift, because I felt like nothing I could find would fix her heart. I simply gave her an honest explanation of what I *wished* I could give her.

~

May 2004

The Daughter She Always Dreamed Of

On this Mother's Day, I wanted to give you something impossible for me to give. Although you have so much to be happy about this year, I know that on this day, you would love to have something more. As this little life inside of me grows and kicks around, I can't help but think of you every time I feel her. I think about how you must have felt every time you felt me kick or turn, and how you probably thought of your mom every time I did something new. I can't imagine not sharing these experiences with you. I know that you wish you could have shared my life with your mom and still have no understanding of why you didn't get to do that. I think about how I want you to be proud of me and watch me grow as I journey through this new phase of life, and it tears my heart out because I know you felt the same way about your mom.

I love to hear you tell me that you love me the way I am and that you know I'm going to be a great mother, but I hate that your mom isn't here to tell you those same things. Every Mother's Day you try to pretend it gets easier, and in some ways maybe it does, but if I lost you right now, I would dread every May for the rest of my life. I wish a daughter could take the place of a mother, but I know that's impossible. So I was thinking about what it is that I am really wanting for you, and this is it:

I want your mom to be here so she can give you what no one else can. I want her to look into your eyes the way you look into mine. I want her to brag about you to her friends and exaggerate how wonderful you really are. I want her to see how hard you try to be all things to all people and tell you it's OK because you're everything to her. I wish she could tell you how proud she is of you for being the greatest mom alive and thank God every day for being blessed with a daughter like you.

I wish she could be there on Sundays to hear you sing. Then you could look out and see her smile over everyone else's and know you were going to be fine. I wish she could carry some of your burdens and listen to you complain about petty little things, because that's what moms do. I wish she could see how strong you are and how you've made it through so many trials in your life. Most of all, above anything else, I wish she could see how much you've loved me and have been everything and more than she taught you to be.

I'm sorry if I've made this Mother's Day harder for you, but I wanted you to know that I cherish everything about you and how amazing you have made my life. I wish your mom could give you all of these things, because you have given them to me. Everything

I'll be as a mother will be because of you, and everything you are is because of her. So I want to thank you both. Because she cannot be here to tell you this, and I know the deep desire in a daughter to make her mother proud, I want to assure you that you are the daughter she always dreamed of!

Happy Mother's Day, Mom!
I love you!

~

I needed to say these things to my mom and tried my best to think of her heart on this day above anything else. I also wrote her a poem to go with it to kind of lighten the mood.

~

May 2004

Your Magic Crayon

I saw a rainbow in the clouds
And thought you must have drawn it

With the magic crayon that you have
And your hands that made everything fit.

I thought there were monsters under my bed
And screamed, but no voice came out.

You came because you knew I had called
And showed me there's nothing to cry about.

I walked in the doors and saw stinky little boys
And wondered why they hadn't combed their hair.

At the end of the day you came back like you promised
And took me home, where I didn't have to share.

I came home crying with a broken heart at ten
And wondered if life would go on

But you made me no-bake chocolate oatmeal cookies
And the next day my troubles were gone.

We've laughed about ice cream falling on the floor
And been embarrassed about closing the broken "boat car's" door.

We've fought about wearing clothes that I hated
And thought of good plans to get rid of guys I dated.

We got excited over swimming in two-foot-shallow pools
And sleeping by the Christmas tree with the lights on.

We hated sharing that last bite of pudding
And ate cookie dough until it was gone.

You made me tents out of blankets and chairs
And always let my friends come play.

You brought me soup, cold rags, Jell-O, and popsicles
And never made me go to school anyway.

You got up at five to make me feel beautiful,
And the list just goes on and on,

But I was wondering, now that I'm going to be a mom,
Could I borrow your magic crayon?

~

Not only was I completely blessed to have an amazing mom and to be able to finally see and appreciate her in ways that I never had before, I also was blessed to have the greatest mother-in-law ever. In June 2004, my home church, Beebe First Assembly of God, had a very special day to honor my mother-in-law, who also had been my pastor's wife since I was five years old. They asked different people to say something that they loved and appreciated about her. I wrote mine down because I'd always had a hard time saying what I wanted to say without it being on paper in front of me, and even then I was always very nervous, to the point of tears, when reading it. But I love this woman so much, and I was honored to get to share my heart this day—shaky voice and all.

~

June 2004

Worthy of Being Honored

Devoted to her family, she overlooks nothing. You can expect that everything important in your life will be graced with her presence and support. She's a woman with few demands. She simply wants to be who she is. She wants to walk into her home knowing that there's a place for everything and everything is in its place. She wants to relax on her couch with a cup of coffee or a bag of popcorn and watch the birds play outside her window. She loves when her kids come to see her. Even if it's only for a few minutes, she takes time to make it a memorable moment in our lives. She loves to bake apple pies and blackberry cobblers and watch our faces as we take that first bite. She loves the feeling of knowing that everything is done for the day and that her only task is to be the wife of the man she has loved for almost forty years.

Yes, she has opinions and frustrations, just like we all do, but I can honestly say this: I've never heard her curse, lie, gossip, or belittle someone's efforts. She has been a wonderful mother, and

I am reaping the benefits of that. She raised a loving, understanding, affectionate, devoted, and determined son, and he is the head of my house. How can I not be blessed?

I would like to say to First Assembly, thank you for allowing her to be who she is. Thank you for loving and honoring her, today and always. To you, Sister Dorsey, mom and friend, thank you for coming into my life. Thank you for sharing your family with me. Thank you for standing up for what you believe in. Thank you for praying for me. Last but not least, thank you for loving me! Because of your devotion to God and his direction for your life, my dreams came true!

I love you!
Suzanne

~

fifteen

Finding Trust

Remember when I told you about the three cousins who are more like brothers to me? Well, the middle one, as I mentioned, was the closest one of all. He was my protector. He was in my circle of friends. He was always in my classes. He was at my lunch. His buddies were my crushes. He was the reason I was never afraid when I got to school. He was smart, strong, confident, and popular, and I always needed him way worse than he needed me. Our bond was pretty unique. He would have done anything for me. He would have given up any friend he had to make sure my heart was OK. I trusted him above anyone. Growing up, we always signed letters to each other, "Your favorite cousin, Me" It was kind of a joke to remind each other "you know you love me most," but in a way, it was true.

After his parents got divorced, his life went downhill. I lived every day to pull him up and keep him out of the pit. I defended him and tried my best to show people the best in him. I believed in him more than anyone else did, and I would not back off until he was safe. In high school, some people do stupid little things that make them look really cool and end up being the things they laugh about at high school reunions while their beautiful wives stand beside them and their wonderful kids are safely at the sitter's. But some people do stupid little things that make them look really cool and then end up destroying their lives. So now, the stupid things they did that attracted their friends in school have driven away their friends as adults, there's no beautiful wife, and they only see their kids if they can get legal rights to them.

Who knows in which direction those stupid *little* things are going to take your life? Don't even roll the dice! It will never be worth it. I saw a church sign yesterday that said, "It's a lot easier to prevent bad habits than it is to break them." I bet no one believes this statement more than my cousin. Like I said earlier, some people you just have to believe in. He is one of those that my heart doesn't know how to give up on.

In October 2004, he was showing signs of turning back to God and changing the direction of his life, but the mind games that had always overtaken him were stopping him from seeing the way out. One day, while praying for him and feeling like I had cried every last tear my body would ever produce, I begged God to show me the way he was thinking so maybe I could understand the struggle he was going through. My heart was flooded with words that I believe were a representation of his heart calling out to mine, to show me where he was and also remind me to never give up. I had *always* been there for him. I had *always* believed in him. I had *always* told him it was possible and that I'd *never* stop holding on to his heart. I knew that he trusted me to never give up on him, and because of that, I trusted him to never stop fighting.

~

October 2004

It's Possible

I know it's there,
But I can't see the sun.
It's like my life
Has no meaning to the world.

I like to close my eyes and dream
That everything I love is near.
I see who I want to be
And all I can see is so clear.

But the rain won't stop
And I've wasted so much time.

You said that I could reach the highest star.
You said that my potential goes so far.
You said that what my life could be is all in my heart
And that it's possible for anyone to start.

Tomorrow is a brand new day.
I'm going to lift my hands and say,
"I love the man I will become,"
And my intentions will be true.

But what if I struggle?
What if I fall?
What if my heart
Has no strength left at all?

Will I ever see the beauty
That somewhere lies in me?

You said that I could reach the highest star.
You said that my potential goes so far.
You said that what my life could be is all in my heart
And that it's possible for anyone to start.

I know the way out
And I know the way in,
But I don't think it's possible
To make this all begin.

I want to see the day.
I want to breathe the air
And make this life of mine
Something people want to share.

You said that I could reach the highest star.
You said that my potential goes so far.
You said that what my life could be is all in my heart
And that it's possible for anyone to start.

I believe in you!
Your favorite cousin, Me

I've tried everything and nothing helps. I'm at the end of my rope. Is there no one who can do anything for me? Isn't that the real question? The answer, thank God, is that Jesus Christ can and does. He acted to set things right in this life of contradictions where I want to serve God with all my heart and mind, but am pulled by the influence of sin to do something totally different.
—Romans 7:21–25 (The Message)

~

There are many questions in life and, sometimes, just as many in the life of a Christian. You pray that God will keep you safe and that your children will be healthy. You pray for families to stay together and for lost loved ones to come back to Jesus. Sometimes, when our prayers are answered like we hoped for, it is encouraging and builds our faith. But what about when they aren't? What do you say when complete and total heartache overtakes a person who did nothing to cause it?

I can look back at my cousin's choices and see the snowball effect that led to where he is today. But what about my friend in ministry who had a baby and five days later had a brain aneurysm that caused her to be completely disabled, leaving her family in total confusion as to what to do next, and not just for the next few months but for the last 15 years, and still today? What about the people who believe, just like I do, that they are living in the favor of God? What about praying for safety? Sometimes it feels pointless.

Opening your heart to honesty will usually give you more than you wanted to find. Sometimes you have to admit that you have doubt. I hate doubting God! It's a total contradiction to my "trust in God" lifestyle, but if we are being honest here, sometimes I have doubt. I don't doubt his existence, but I doubt his choices or what looks like absence in my time of need. And every time I do, I'm reminded that my ways are not God's ways and my thoughts are not his thoughts. I know that he can see the bigger picture, where it all makes sense, and if I could see the bigger picture, it would scare me to death and make me doubt even more.

We always want to know what God has for our future. We want it all to make sense. We think that if God would just tell us what things are going to be like, and spell it all out for us, we would be able to trust him. Here's what I have to say about that now. What if God had said all of this?

"Suzanne, will you marry Jason Dorsey and submit to him in all of his decisions to follow me? Will you move to Springfield and become very close to a girl who, because of human circumstances, will have a brain aneurysm two years later and never be able to speak to you again? You won't ever understand why it happened, but I need you to trust me and know that, no matter what, I am with you and I am with her.

"Will you then go to a church and be a youth pastor's wife where you will start with ten kids who, for the most part, do not want to be at church and will not accept you until you are almost finished with the assignment, and where you will feel like you are giving much more than you receive to lives that you will have to leave after nineteen months? You will feel inadequate and overwhelmed most of the time. To make ends meet, you will have to work a full-time job, where you will work with some very dramatic women who will cause you to feel nervous most of the time, and you will wish that every work day would be over before it ever starts, mostly because you will be running around like crazy with all the church events after work is over, and you will always feel exhausted.

"Will you then go back to your home church and take a lot of criticism from people who (you will feel) see you as 'just one of us and trying to *act* like you're called of God,' but will you love them no matter what comes your way?

"Oh, by the way, you know all that stuff in your past that made you fear every moment of the day? Well, you will be doing all of this ministry work while dealing with it. Eventually, you will lose some of your friends to the very life that together you and they used to fight to save others from. You will feel betrayed and heartbroken. You will feel embarrassed and wonder how many people could now believe *you* were ever real, seeing the life that your own armor-bearers are now so proudly living to only please themselves.

"Will you then become a missionary to the public school campuses of Arkansas, where you will mostly have to send Jason off by himself, and you will feel lonely, sad, and bitter at times because the only way you can get support for this ministry, or even do this ministry, is by him traveling? I will provide for your needs, and you will have me by your side, every moment, but you will have no extra. You won't be able to go shopping much at all. Your heart will sink every time your truck is on empty because gas at that time will be basically unaffordable. You will shop at secondhand stores if you decide to buy anything for yourself. You will have just enough the entire time, and you will live this way for at least eleven years and maybe more.

"You know how you always wanted to be a mom and have what you think is the perfect little family, with two boys and one girl, with two perfect years in between each child? Try three girls...in four years...while developing hypothyroidism, Meniere's disease, extreme hormonal imbalances, and moving nine times in your first fourteen years of marriage. Feeling like you redefined the definition of zombie, you will forget what a full night's sleep feels like. Though you will be the one to take care of your daughters the many times that their daddy just can't be there, he will be their hero and this won't always feel good to your excited little heart.

"All of your close friends will have moved far away. You won't be able to go to one single church frequently enough to be close to anyone—if you want to be able to travel with your husband, that is. You won't have people coming over to your house or be invited to theirs for game nights or dinner very often because of your lack of involvement in their lives. You will feel like you belong to everyone but somehow *no one*. Most people will think you have lots of friends because of all the acquaintances you will have, but you will actually have very few. You'll also find out that the greatest role models and friends you ever had, whom you trusted more than anyone in life, will go through something that will tear your heart into a million pieces and leave you wondering if there's anyone you can ever trust again.

"Are you willing to live this life? If I tell you how many souls will be saved and how many lives will be touched...if I tell you how many women, kids, and even men will watch the way you handle it all...that they will see how, in your weakness, I am strong and be encouraged daily...Will you do it now?

"How about if I tell you that many people will come to you because you will understand where they are and that your heart will have the compassion that they need to see a hope-filled future, even in the middle of their deepest pain? Is that enough?

"What if I tell you that you will look back someday and never wish you'd had a different life? What if I say, 'Someday, still having only the bare necessities, you will see yourself as the richest woman alive'?

"What if I can show you how it will all work together for the good and how you will begin to see that life without struggles is life without victories? Even if I tell you it will all make sense in the end, will you, being eighteen years old with a broken heart and no way to see or believe in the process of my plan, now trust me and live this life?"

If God had said *that* to me, I would have been completely overwhelmed, confused, hurt, and terrified. *I* was marrying the man of my dreams. *I* had the perfect dress and the perfect wedding! *I* had obeyed God all my life! *I* was about to be happy and blessed! All of those things were true, but there was no way, in the state I was in, I could have accepted the struggles coming my way, even knowing the outcome, without actually walking through the *process* of it all. Saying that to you breaks my heart, but saying it at all gives me so much assurance in a God whose thoughts are not my thoughts and whose ways are so much higher than my ways!

In our lives of faith, trusting God's ways and simply saying, "Yes, Lord," no matter what we face or don't understand, has to be enough—if we want to live out our purpose, that is. I'm so glad I didn't know about my tomorrows, because my yesterdays might have kept me from believing I could face what was ahead.

We can never see God as the one who is standing on the other side of the ocean, "waiting with open arms," and wonder how in the world we can ever make it to him. He is the one right in front of us along the way. He is not concerned about the waves or the wind blowing us in the wrong direction every now and then because he knows how to get us to our destination no matter how many times we get off track. He only wants to be our guide through it all. Some of my favorite lyrics, by Scott Krippayne, are, "Sometimes he calms the storm with a whispered peace: 'Be still.' He can settle any sea, but it doesn't mean he will. Sometimes he holds us close and lets the wind and waves go wild. Sometimes he calms the storm, and other times he calms his child." This isn't always easy to accept, and often it creates doubt for those around us who are looking for any chance to say, "Uh-huh, where is your God now?" But because I now know what it feels like to conquer a storm, and what that can do for the people around me, I can honestly say, "I would rather be held in the arms of God through a storm than to *ever* have him stop it!" Doubt or no doubt, the peace in my heart wins.

I refuse to live my life to *prove* God right or wrong. I believe in God because of my relationship with him. I can look back on every day of my life and show you where God stepped in and saved my heart. When I would walk down those halls and know the things that were being said about me, which should have forced me into rage, God was there. At my church, with girls who had no reason to hate me but found so many ways to make me feel discouraged, God was there. In my own home, when the fighting was relentless and pride ruled us all, God was there. Every night that I lay down on my pillow and cried, "God, help me go to sleep fast so I won't be scared! God, take this pain out of my heart! God, show me how to be like you! I can't do this anymore!" he was there. If my life were a movie and spiritual things could be seen, you would see God right there with me, in every moment of every day.

Could God have spared me from it all? Yes, but how would I be who I am without it? It is so hard to let your kids go through the things you know they need to learn from and grow from, even when you can see the benefit of it, because you don't want them to feel that pain of it. You choose to do it anyway because you know it's what they need. You are the one who's there every day, the one who knows them. You know how to not push them too far and not hold on too tight. You are the one who knows what they can handle. You know how much is too much. As much as parents love their children and know what has to happen for them to learn, how much more does God know what we need to face and what we need to be spared from? No one knew me better than God. No one loved me more than God. Because he never leaves me, and in every moment I can feel where he is, I believe in him.

I believe the Bible is the inspired word of God, and I can't imagine my life without it, but I don't believe in God because of the Bible. I can look back over my life and give you testimony after testimony of times God has come through for me. I was even healed of really bad scoliosis as a child. The doctor said my spine looked like a question mark, and I'd have to be put in a brace that would come up over my head and that I'd have to wear to school every day. I was prayed for and, the next day, went back to the doctor, who did not believe in miracles (at that time). He was in shock and said, "Your spine is as straight as a board. I don't understand it!" Never wore a brace one day in my life. Never had another problem with my spine!

I can also tell you of many times that I felt like God was refusing to answer my prayers and I was straight-up ticked off because I thought he didn't even care. I didn't always like what he had to say, but his presence and his peace were security for my heart when I had none. Presence and peace are unexplainable but are something I could talk about all day long. I am probably the worst person to debate the existence of God with because his constant presence and his overwhelming peace are my main reasons for believing in him and trusting in his ways. They are also reasons you can't take away and you can't prove wrong, no matter how many scientific arguments there are.

"A man with an experience is never at the mercy of the man with an argument." —Amy Sollars

Nothing in my life or in the lives of those around me, even with my many doubts and fears, has pulled me further from believing that God loves me and has my best interest at heart. Everything that has happened in my life, though extremely hard at times, has shown me my purpose and my reason for existing. The pain and struggles aren't necessarily what I would have chosen for myself. They opened so many doors for me to run. *But fighting against every instinct to not follow God only made me that much more determined to follow him!* Even if there are times we follow God because it's a challenge, I feel safe in saying, "Keep on winning. Eventually your heart will reap the benefits of the race!"

Hard times? Yes. Great times? Yes. Walking any day alone? Not a single one. Only God can take my heart and keep it safe when everyone around me *seems* to fail me, when life is against me, when I don't understand, when I am my biggest enemy, and when I'm at the end of my strength. I doubt a lot of things, but not one time have I doubted that God is with me.

When my husband messes up, in my eyes, and does something different from what I think is best, I get mad and I voice my opinion. I never for one second doubt that he loves me, and do you know why? Because he's always there. He always has my best interest at heart. In our ministry, he can handle my frustration and anger when he knows more about the situation than me. It makes sense to him *why* I am mad. He understands what I'm feeling, but he is still responsible for doing what's right. I hate not winning with my point of view, but I can handle him being right, even when I wish things were different, because his unconditional love and devotion to me allows me to trust him. I know that as long as I'm with him, it's going to be OK. Even if the situation is not OK, I am with him. He will never leave me or turn his back on me. If all that people ever see in the middle of conflict is abandonment, I don't know how they can ever believe in the unconditional love of God. I'm so thankful that no matter what comes my way, my life with my husband only proves God's hand on my life and his love for me, more and more and more.

It's a really good thing that the above paragraph is 100 percent true because *life* continued to happen. One day as I was praying for another good friend (also in ministry) and her son, I became very upset and started writing, "Trust" (from the perspective of the mom). This perfectly healthy little boy had developed an infection in his brain that resulted in permanent brain damage and put him in the hospital for many weeks. I had just had my baby girl a few months prior and couldn't imagine this happening to her. I kept asking God, "Why? Why do things like this happen to babies and to people who are in ministry, giving you their entire lives? I know we are human bodies, but can't you fix this? God, why would you not fix this?"

My "why" was not answered that day, but I really felt like God spoke to me as I began to write. As you read this next poem, remember one of two things: If your children are healthy, *thank God*, and never take for granted the moments you share with them. If your children aren't healthy, thank God that you were given the gift of life, and that you were never expected to deal with hard times on your own!

Sometimes I know God says, "Really? You really think you'd depend on me if you had no pain, no hurt, not conflicts? You really think that ministers should be exempt from tragedy, all the while trying to relate to hurting people?" And most of all, *to me*, I think God says, "Please step out of the way with all of your thinking and dwelling and questions and 'if I were God, I would...' and just love people!" For me, that's a very hard one. I am so glad God doesn't get mad when I don't understand. He gently tells me to get out of the way and somehow uses that to make me love and trust him even more.

~

October 2004

Trust

How will I ever see
The good in all of this?
So many things I'd waited for
Are now the things I miss.

That sparkle in his eyes,
The sound of his sweet voice—
I know that God is not to blame,
But why is healing not his choice?

When I kiss him, I can feel
His heart loving mine.
I don't know how, It all seems so hard,
But he's going to be just fine.

Is it like the day I brought him home
And his eyes could hardly see me?
But I held him and fed him and smiled
Because I knew my baby boy he would always be.

Can you really say
That "unfortunate" is how you now see me
Because you've never held him in your arms
And you don't know what his future will be?

Yes, I'm sad and angry
And confused all in one.
I've cried and prayed and believed for so long
That my faith is almost gone.

But if God is God—
And I know that he is—
Somehow, someway,
He will fix all of this,

Maybe like I want him to.
Wouldn't that be nice?
But I've got to trust that he knows best
Without thinking twice.

My prayers are different than they used to be
And there's so much hurt inside me,
But every day I'm reminded
That I'm not in control and never will be.

~

I sure wish I could tell you how God completely healed that little boy, but he didn't. I could, however, write another book titled *Aftereffect* and give you story after story of how God has used this family to reach out and be an example to thousands of others whom life has dealt a bad hand. Is it getting easier to trust God when I don't understand? Yes. Is this family a huge reason I do trust God in the middle of my doubts? Yes! I'm not saying it was God's will for this little boy to be permanently brain damaged or that God will not someday heal him. I'm simply saying that either way, God is with them. Because of that reason alone, their hearts and thousands of others' will be OK. People may be looking for answers to their problems, but when they see that their *courage* was actually the *answer someone* else needed, it will change the way they see problems all together.

Trust in the Lord with all your heart and lean not on your own understanding; in all your ways acknowledge him, and he will make your paths straight. —Proverbs 3:5–6 (NIV)

sixteen

Finding Joy

~

December 2004

Your Life

I remember when I saw the top of your head coming from me. You came giving no pain to my body (with a little help from the medicine). Your eyes immediately saw your daddy, and I expected nothing different. He had been talking, singing, praying over you, tapping to teach you rhythm all along your journey inside of me. You always responded to his voice, and as soon as you were born, you heard that voice that had been telling you who you were before you were ever born. Even after the whole family came in and there were many voices in the room, when you heard his voice, you literally turned your head his way.

I was somewhat in shock. People always said I wouldn't know the feeling until I had it. That is so true, and I still can't put it into words. Every time I see another mother with a newborn, I want to say, "Isn't it the greatest thing in the world?" I remember how you would suck on my finger. I can still feel it! I heard something on TV that explains the way I felt: "The first time I saw you I forgot to breathe!"

Once everyone had left the hospital and it was just you, Daddy and me, we were in the bed holding you, and you looked right at us! They say it takes a few days for babies to focus, but we knew you were seeing us at that moment, and no one could tell us different. We will never forget those dark-blue eyes that stared deep into ours. It felt like the whole world just stopped for about thirty seconds. I don't know if it was miraculous or if some babies actually can see clearly when they are born, but I know it happened. It felt like God's way of giving me a moment I'll never forget—when our hearts connected for the first time.

You are four months old, and this is the first thing I have written about you. People have asked me if I have written any poems to you or about you, and I have had to tell them no. It seems like I would have a thousand things to write about and a million feelings to express. That's just it—there are so many things to say that it's impossible to lump them all into one, two, or even ten writings.

I could sit down and write about your every sound! I could tell of the way my heart breaks every time you smile at me. I could express my feelings every moment of every day, and it still would not tell of the love I have for you. This is my first attempt on paper to say what your life means to me.

Cooper, I love the way you smell. When you're not here, I smell your blankets, and I stand in your room imagining the second you will get home. I love the way you laugh and squeal. I love looking at your hundreds of pictures (even your ultrasound pictures) and reliving every moment that you have been alive. I love the way you yawn and almost always give an "uhhhhh" at the end of it. I love the way you rub your nose on my shoulder and how you hold your head up to look around. I love to hear you talking to yourself when you wake up in the mornings, and I love the way you smile at me when I come to get you out of bed. I even love the way you cry.

I love your belly, your toes, and the way your eyes are smiling even when your mouth is not. I love how curious you are and how, when you hear music, you always look to see what it is. I love how you splash your feet in the bathtub and how you always smile when I wrap you up in the towel. I love holding you right after you have eaten and are too full to move around. I love when you put your face against mine, and I love the way you try to walk when I hold you up, like you think you really can.

I haven't recorded every single event, date, time, and place. I haven't written on the back of every picture. I've probably lost a few socks and wasted a lot of formula since you've been born, but everything I wanted to do in my life that matters most, I have done. I have lived a devoted life to God and to my parents. I have married my best friend, who just happens to be the man of my dreams. I have felt a "life" inside of me! And I have held in my arms the most beautiful, happy, healthy baby girl, who will some-day call me Mommy. Even though you had no control over exist-ing, thank you for being born and for making my dreams come true.

I love you, Cooper Rae Dorsey, and I always will!

~

For each hard time that came my way, there were at least a thousand good times. And once I became a mommy, I soon began to forget the bad. Kids have a way of taking all that makes life hard, including their own raising, and making it worth every struggle! I hope to share more about that in another book, but oh, how my life has taken off in a new direction ever since August 4, 2004.

Being the happy mother of a new baby, my time was completely filled with all that was "Cooper"! We were out and about every single day. I was the proudest mom you could have ever known! I did everything I had been dreaming of for...well, basically all my life. We read books and studied colors and shapes every day. We watched Baby Einstein videos and named out loud everything we saw. We didn't leave home without the whole nursery packed into one backpack (which was *not* pink but black so Jason could carry it too). We sang in the car, we ate on schedule, we slept on schedule, our clothes matched every moment of the day, and we kept all the toys sanitized. She went to stay with her grandparents on a regular basis, and she fell completely in love with them. Mommy and Daddy got to have date nights at least once or twice a month! Every time my parents brought her home, it felt like I was seeing her for the first time, over and over and over again. It was a *dream* world!

These are the moments that I will remember all of my life. Every picture I see from the first year of Cooper's life, I can close my eyes and be there in an instant. I tell her all the time, "You are my dream come true!" She really is. Waiting makes you anxious, and once you experience the joy that takes all of that away, in one second, you just have to sit back and thank God for every moment along the way, good and bad.

When Cooper was about ten months old, something very good and very bad happened. It was hard to know how to feel about it. The job that my dad had for eighteen years was no longer going to be a man's job but a computer's. The people he worked with made his life miserable, but the money was good, and he was devoted, even to something he hated, because he took pride in everything he did. On the one hand, what happened would free up my dad for the first time ever to give his time to the people who needed him—himself, my mom, me, and now his granddaughter, whom he absolutely adored. On the other hand, he would be losing security, insurance, retirement, fulfillment, and a part of his dignity.

Because Father's Day was coming up right around the corner, and I thought the world of my dad, I wanted to give him something that would honor him. He had been at this job for so long, and I felt like he deserved to be recognized, at least for the fact that he'd given them such a big part of his life. Of course, I am biased about my own father, but you could go ask any man there about my dad, and if he were honest, he would tell you what a great man and hard worker my dad was! I knew they were not going to honor him with words or anything else but I sure had some words for them. I didn't go up there and give those men this poem, but I thought about it, and I definitely wanted my dad to hear the words that I wrote of him.

~

June 2005

The Man They Never Saw

Only you will ever know
The sacrifices made.
You're the one who understands
The prices that were paid.

To be the man they never saw,
The one they never knew,
The best they could've asked for
Was right there in plain view.

To give someone so much of life
Devotion unworthy of,
You truly must be the greatest of all.
Your heart must be sent from above.

Of course, there were days when no one knew
The pain that you were dealt

Except the one who created you:
Your pain He always felt.

You deserve a crown of perseverance
And one of honesty,
A robe of faithfulness,
And a monument for being so trustworthy.

If they never see what they've lost—
Although I know they will—
Without realizing that they are,
They'll look for something "real."

"Another Dale Gibbons, perhaps," they'll ponder,
But only time will reveal
That God made one man to be like you,
And sorrow they'll begin to feel.

Your prayers were never unheard
And your tears were never wasted.
God has a plan now: your time there has ended,
But their souls, because of you, have plainly tasted

Just how good God really is
And how He'll make a way.
Even though you are no longer with them,
A piece of your heart will stay.

Reminding them, even ones you never told,
That life is only what you make it,
And happiness comes only by wearing
The shoes that actually fit.

They'll see that you believed in yourself
Enough to look fear in the face,

And that courage to do what you did today
Came only because of God's grace.

You can live your life beaten down,
But what glory can God receive?
Even when life doesn't make much sense,
In Him you must believe.

So they will see that who you are
Is not the man they know
But that God in you
Makes you more than your life could ever show.

Be careful what you say and be careful what you do.
The one you find no use for may be the only one praying for you.
Your reasoning, I'll never know. Finding out, I'll never bother.
But oh, if you could have known that man, that man who is my father!

I love you, Dad! Even if you never receive honor from those who owe you so much, always know that you're my hero, and without your love in my heart, I'd be nothing!

—Suzanne

~

I wish that my dad could see the good in the things that sometimes only look bad. It's been a battle for him. Though I cannot change that for him, it makes me fight hard to find the joy in all of my moments. When you are left with "sink" or "swim without a life jacket" as your two options, sometimes even the way you would not have chosen becomes beautiful.

Happiness is a choice that you have to make by accepting joy as your *only* option. I didn't always have that perspective. I wanted what I wanted and thought I couldn't be happy without it. Having Cooper was, thankfully, the way God showed me what pure, perfect joy really feels like. Understanding the difference between having joy and having an acceptance of what life brought my way was exactly what I needed to make joy my priority, at all costs.

God doesn't give us what we *want* to make us happy. He gives us what we *need* so that we can understand what happiness really is. It just so happened that in this case, I got to have both.

seventeen

Finding Peace

Not growing up in ministry, I had a lot of preconceived ideas about it. I thought people were going to love me, look up to me, and hold me in the highest place of their hearts. I thought there would be trips, banquets, fancy clothes, and plenty of dinner partners to go out to eat with. I thought there would be a network of people who always understood where I was and wanted to be with me no matter what. No one told me this was what it would be like. That's just what I had always thought about the people who were in ministry over me. I placed them on high pedestals and thought their lives were pretty much perfect. I saw peace and joy in their faces. I saw victorious, beautiful lives, and I wanted that for myself. I didn't go into ministry because of these reasons—I was simply answering the call of God on my life—but it's still what I thought I was getting into (remember...eighteen years old, very gullible me).

I quickly realized people are people, no matter what. Even my perfect husband wasn't always perfect. He sure was close, though, and he was everything that I wanted to be. It's hard to live with someone like him and not constantly want him to be around. I'm not a wife who waits for the times her husband is gone so she can be herself. I am myself most when my husband is beside me.

We had been missionaries for a year, and all my preconceived ideas about ministry had been completely tossed out the window. I realized that the reality of loving people is that you will be hurt.

You will not always be loved back. You will not always wear fancy clothes. Sometimes, no one will want to be with you, and there will be times that you aren't even meant to be with the people you are ministering to. Wow...very hard to swallow.

Many times as missionaries, we've had to surrender to the fact that it's just not going to be easy. Many times, I find myself thinking, "And I thought church ministry was hard! Being missionaries is even harder! At least when you are on staff at a church, you have people that are always there and a few people that always want *you* there." But obeying the call of God does not put you in the middle of Easy Street, and getting hung up on how bumpy the road can be will only cause your trip to seem harder. Sometimes, all you can do is focus on the people you are picking up along the way and thank God that he is using you to pick them up. If life got to be about "me" for everyone, who would be reaching out to anyone? For those who want life to be all about them, they will never find true contentment. We were created in the image of God. God is love. Love doesn't say, "Me first. You second." Some may think pleasing themselves is the only way to have peace but that couldn't be further from the truth. I believe this with all my heart, and can testify that there's no other way to have true peace inside than to love the way God loves.

Through all of our years in ministry, God has done a completely different work inside of me than he has inside of Jason but has somehow made it all fit together. I'm always amazed at how creatively he can do that. Like I said before, I've had many great moments, and they far outweigh the bad, but on a day like I was having in September 2005, when I was missing my best friend, my encourager, my tag-team partner, and the love of my life, I couldn't hold it in anymore. I had also learned that saying how I truly felt was the only way to release those feelings so that I could see with clearer vision—God's vision.

~

September 2005

In Your Arms

Sometimes I feel bitter and resentful,
But then I realize I'm just confused.
I see the need and it's great, I agree,
But my best friend I don't want to lose.

If I was given one single day
To have all my dreams come true,
I'd simply ask for one single thing:
To spend twenty-four hours with you.

Maybe I'm overreacting,
Exaggerating probably,
But today as I cry and stop the tears,
In your arms is where I want to be.

You can't be everywhere at once.
If possible, you'd be the first to achieve it.
You're the most amazing man in the world.
Of you everyone needs a little bit.

It usually doesn't bother me like this,
And my heart just goes right along beating,
But today I want them all to go away
And have you to myself with no one asking.

I'm tired from not sleeping, my head is pounding,
And my broken heart is hurting my chest,
But I know we will make it, 'cause we always do,
And my smile will be just like the rest.

Thankful that this hard time in our life is over,
If only for two or three days,
And blessed to be the one you love more than any—
That's what my smile and my heart will say.

I love you because you're the man of my dreams,
And no one could ever take your place.
If it's today or tomorrow, I'll anxiously wait
Until my eyes see the beauty of your face.

~

When Jason walks through the door, I take a deep breath. It's not because I want him to take over or help out, though that's so nice to have. It's because the rest of me catches up with what's left of me. He completes me. He brings out the best in me. When I couldn't see life the way it was meant to be, he's the one who showed me. When my idea of ministry failed me, he made it my way to find the *real* Jesus. When my fears were my handicap, he showed me how to make them my victories. When my criticism was the only way I knew, he showed me how to use it to find the good in people. When I think I'm failing, he shows me a hundred ways I'm winning. When I hate the part inside of me that I can't take out, he covers it up with everything he loves about me. Even when I'm wrong, and it means he gets the short end of the stick, he uses it to teach me grace.

Jason is the reason I was able to begin my journey to freedom from a broken heart, without even realizing it. He was with me every single time. He read every single word I wrote, and he encouraged me to say each of them, assuring me that no matter what came of it, he would stand beside me and in front of me if necessary. Obviously there were many other very personal things I had to say to people around me, and I couldn't share them all. I don't think he always agreed with everything I said, but he had a way of using it to teach me, "Maybe you should pray about that some more and make sure it's God and not you." Every day was a life lesson with him. It was exhausting but it was the road I had to take. God knew that Jason Dorsey was the man for me!

eighteen

Finding Freedom

Though the last poem in this book was written in September 2005, God had me wait eight years after that to finally complete it. I went back at least a hundred times and read through the things my heart needed to say. Then I would look at where I was that day and see how God used each moment of my life to bring me to the next place and then the next place. It was like every day God was taking another piece of my heart and gluing it back to the rest of the pieces. I'm so glad he kept up with all of the pieces. I wouldn't have known where to even start looking for them.

When my heart was full of pain, it was all I could see. It blurred my vision with everyone I knew. Even the people who were good for me were viewed in a negative light. I stayed critical because I hated myself and felt like every word said was against me. I stayed offended because the pain I refused to let go of kept reminding me that it might happen again. I stayed sad. I learned to love my self-pity because it was the one thing that I could control and that had always been there for me. I thought I was the *only* one who understood myself, and it felt pointless to try to explain me to anyone else. I wondered why love was not fixing my heart.

I stayed weak because I was afraid that being strong meant I would have to change, and change was the one thing I was sick of. I craved stability and peace, but the lies I'd learned to tell myself were that this was who I was and who I would always be, so I should just accept it. Basically, I allowed no room for healing because I was on a spinning hamster wheel of pain and couldn't figure out how to get off. I only knew how to stay on.

If you can muster up the courage to be honest and let it out, no matter what the outcome will be, you will no longer feel trapped by the people who may or may not even know they are trapping you. Once you realize that God can restore you, you will no longer see him as one more person who abandoned you—he will be the one who never left. That in itself is healing—not to mention the way God continues to fill in the gaps every single time you make room inside your heart for him. Your joy is then no longer up to the actions or reactions of others because you begin to experience true peace that no one in this world can give you or take away from you.

God began to prepare my heart to make all of this public knowledge; he would use it to help many people around the world who felt trapped by something they couldn't explain.

I was so excited to share the things God had shown me but very nervous because of the intensity of some of my feelings. The last thing I wanted to do was cause more pain and confusion in my family, but God assured me that the purpose of the book was far greater than any criticism I would face. I realized that opening my heart to a hurting world, and especially to the people I loved most, would only be healing for us all.

I love my life. I know trials are on the way. I also know victories will follow. I know that my family loves me and that all of the pain we have been through is only going to be for someone else's good—in many ways, for mine as well. I believe I have a purpose. I believe that God can take *any* story and give it a happy ending. I see clearly! I see with eyes of grace. It's so amazing to live in freedom, love with an honest heart, and experience true joy because I tell you the truth.

~

September 2005

Because I Tell You the Truth

Did I make you laugh? Did I make you cry?
Did I make you sit down and wonder why
You've never said how you truly feel
And admitted that your emotions are really real?

Did you think it was harsh
To warn them of death?
Did your heart pound faster?
Did you run out of breath?

Were you scared
I might make a small thing big
Or a face turn red
Or a dead love live?

Did you call me disrespectful
And later understand?
Are you happy that you know me?
Are you glad you took my hand?

Because I tell you the truth:
I can always be me.
I'll never have to fear
That my heart is what you'll see.

It may hurt at times
And it may even bleed,
But if you'll listen to my heart,
Time is all you'll need.

When you love without ceasing and hold on without releasing,
Nothing can break the ties.
We don't love because it feels good or commit because we're told
we should.
Our hearts never part: no good-byes.

Whether words to tell
Of the love you feel
Or the pain inside
Or the hope that's real,

Your heart must speak them out.
Never expect someone to understand
Until they know what you're all about.

No regrets of choices made,
No sorrow for games not played,
No fear of where my head I will lay,
No wishing for a different day,

Every prayer in some way answered,
Every question eventually understood:
I can see my life as wonderful
Because my God was always good.

I will not say I'm sorry for my honesty,
Not one bit.
I have a life of happiness:
All the pieces fit.

Not a day goes by when I don't wish
I could make the whole world brighter,
But it's not up to me to say how they feel.
I can't make their load any lighter.

Tell me one more time what it is you're dreaming of,
And I'll tell you the same as before:
Peace will come when you take the keys *you* are holding
And open honesty's door.

~

Made in the USA
Charleston, SC
10 September 2014